CODING GAMES

*TIPS AND TRICKS TO MASTER
THE KEY CONCEPTS OF CODING*

ROBERT C. MATTHEWS

Table of Contents

Introduction 1

Chapter 1: What is Coding? 4

    Our Dumb Smartphones 6

    Types of Programming Languages 13

    Compilers 15

    Hybrid Translators 15

    Assemblers 16

    Why Should I Learn Coding? 17

    Types Of Coders 21

Chapter 2: Concepts Of Programming 33

    Control Structures 43

    Data Structures 66

    Syntax 74

Chapter 3: Coding Games 79

    Robocode: What is Robocode? 79

    CodeCombat 95

    What is CodeCombat? 96

    Using CodeCombat in a Coding Curriculum 97

CodeMonkey.. 107

4 SQL Murder Mystery 114

Elevator Saga 115

Untrusted.. 116

Flexbox Defense 116

CodinGame 117

Chapter 4: Programming Languages....................................... 118

HTML... 118

JAVA.. 134

PYTHON 139

Conclusion 146

Introduction

L et's face it; coding isn't fun. I mean, yeah we all know what the web and the glamorous designs and the "become a master in 2 weeks!" flashy ads that pop up on the computers say, but you and I both know the truth. It isn't right. It's tedious and boring and arrgh. Sounds fair and true, right? Except for one little thing - it isn't.

When learned in a stifled, rigid manner, coding can seem like one of the most tedious tasks in the world, with tons of meaningless instructions and no foreseeable ending in sight. However, when learned in a more relaxed atmosphere, accompanied by the right amount of motivation and inspiration, learning to code significantly improves in outlook. It changes from something that makes you want to bash your head against the wall in frustration, to something that makes you want to hit the ceiling in wild joy. Okay, perhaps that's a *little teeny* bit of an exaggeration but you get the point. Either way your head still suffers from bashing while learning to code. And it can be so much fun.

How so? What is this right environment I speak of, you wonder? Well I'd tell you but before I continue, I must warn you not to scoff. If you're going to, best not to read this book. But if you're game, well, the answer is right up there. Games.

Yes, games. Despite your elitist leanings, negative stereotyping and all the things you have been taught about the evils of levity and games in serious affairs, games can greatly boost your assimilation of coding concepts. They can, nay, *will*, turn you to a better programmer faster over time than if you went at it without. In this case, business and pleasure do mix - and unless you are different from the norm, this is likely to be the only pleasure you're going to be getting from your proficiency in programming.

The game-based learning method is already gaining serious ground in different sectors, ranging from health to finance and business. Even with medical schools and other sectors of learning, now prefer to disperse pertinent information via the gaming method, as opposed to the age-old method of traditional torturing, I mean, lecturing. These games are made through coding, by the way. It seems only rational to extend the practice of learning through coded games to coding itself.

However, although games aren't just stupid time-wasting contraptions and if properly optimized, can be a great source of learning, they are also not the most helpful educational material out there. Indeed, you shouldn't jump straight into coding games, without first an understanding (however rough) of coding. Remember the coding games are supposed to *aid* you in your programming journey. They are not by themselves the source of learning. After all, a ton of fertilizer can do nothing if you do not plant the seed in it.

Hence, in this book, we will first begin with a brief overview of what programming is, its history (it's not as bad as it sounds. I promise!) and the fundamental concepts all programming languages rely on. Next we'll mention the different programming languages there are and go in-depth in some selected ones. Next, we will list the different coding games out there, explaining how they work, what programming languages they teach and what they focus on.

And finally, we'll teach you how to game the games, and use them to boost your coding journey. After all, as Albert Einstein famously *didn't* say, "Everything I know, I learned from games". Or something to that effect

We have a lot to discuss. Let us begin.

Chapter 1

What is Coding?

The year is 2205. The earth is peaceful. We've unlocked all great secrets and current mysteries still troubling us - poverty, cancer, space travel, whether a tree falling in the forest makes a sound. Everything is going well. Oh, and the Queen is still alive. Things couldn't get any better.

So they don't. In fact, they take a surprising twist when an unidentified flying object crashes into a sleepy suburban town in North America (because, obviously, that's where they all land). After tense deliberations from all concerned parties, the Government decides to send a team of specialists to determine the level of threat the ship poses because err… you know how it goes.

And so they go, this team, and instead of the whole Hollywood blockbuster scene coursing through your mind right now, they discover something completely different indeed. They discover that these new aliens truly do "come in peace" and can do so many wonderful things. *Very* many wonderful things, in fact, all designed to make our lives easier and so much better than it is right now. There is just one snag, however. One teeny tiny little problem stopping these wonderful aliens (whom we shall now call for future references Sirexa) from being the green fairy angel sent by Mother Milky Way-they didn't speak our language.

Not only that. Even worse, they required a completely and explicitly stated instruction in "their" own tongue to carry out an instruction. If you said for example to them, "water", while choking on something, you'd receive nothing but confused silence. Even if you said "Can I get a cup of water", still silence.

In fact, unless you say to them,

> *"Go to the kitchen, take a cup made of glass, sorry, a cup made from a mixture of silicon dioxide, limestone and calcium carbonate from the pantry, proceed to the kitchen sink, and at the kitchen sink, twist the tap to the side until dihydrogen monoxide comes out then stop. Put the glass to the mouth of the sink and remain stationary until the dihydrogen monoxide liquid occupies a significant volume not less than 75% in the cup. Next, turn the tap opposite to the direction it was initially turned in and stop when water, I mean, dihydrogen monoxide liquid stops dripping from the sink. Finally, return in the direction you came from with the cup in your hand and bring it to me",*

You're likely not going to get any water from them. Or, even worse, they might misinterpret your instructions, and attack a dam or something. Hence, carefulness.

And what a dilemma. For a resource so magnificent, with immense potential to completely reshape the world being so needlessly clumsy, and requiring extremely precise language to carry out even the simplest of tasks. A truly frustrating scenario indeed.

However, humanity is not dampened much by the situation. Indeed, there is merely quiet optimism when such news spread across some quarters.

You see, humanity has faced such complications, the complication of extremely precise writing in a completely different language with very little margin of error lest the whole thing crashes. Yes, humanity has faced such aliens before. Only they went by a different name. Their names were computers.

Our Dumb Smartphones

"Okay, nice story, but what does this have to do with coding?" a doubting Thomas might ask. Well, as it will soon turn out, nothing and everything.

Because here's the deal about laptops, computers and smartphones. They are very dumb. All of them. Dumb. Completely, physically stupid. Denser than a cloud of Sulphur. Thicker than a bar of lead. More obtuse than President Trum-. Alright, I think you get the point.

But again, despite the obtuse nature of these devices, here is one thing we all know.

Computers and smartphones are *amazing*. Without doubt the best perk of living in the modern world. With one click, we can do so many things that would have been considered sorcery just 60 years ago. And rightly so. With just one click, we can access unlimited troves of information, connect with millions around the globe and just generally do........anything! You can monitor real-time news in Pakistan while watching a concert in Paris sitting peacefully in your home in Australia just after ordering a book from North America. The breathless possibilities and wondrous applications of the internet and machine technology in literally every single sector of our lives are almost infinite. Without exaggerating, smartphones and computers are literally the most important feature and driving force of this age.

Now, all this sounds nice and the potentials and applications sound wondrous. And indeed it is. Except for one teeny tiny little problem, two in fact. Computers and smartphones, as earlier said, are dumb. Very, *very* dumb. So dumb in fact that they have to be told in extremely specific instructions what to do or else they will fail to execute said task. Even worse, a poorly stated or ambiguous instruction could lead to dangerous consequences such as lax loopholes which can lead to your computer doing the very opposite of what you want at the very least. At worst, a huge flaming undead army of robots looking to enslave the whole of humanity and even worse, indoctrinate them with cute cat videos 24/7. Okay, maybe not that bad. But you get the point.

The second problem is that despite what the friendly interface wants you to believe, Computers do not speak English. Or French. Or German. Or Vulcan. In fact, as it turns out, computers and mobile devices do not speak any language known to man. Yet (because, hey, Terminator). Instead, these machines converse only in incredibly boring segues and a series of 1's and 0's, known as *binary*.

Why can't computers understand us, and why do they talk only with binary? Well, a lot of reasons have been offered, but the leading theory I believe, as of writing this book, is that it's because these internet machines are......*machines*.

That mystery aside, there then exists, as you might have noticed, a huge problem.

On the one hand, you have these wonderful computers, smartphones and tablets able to perform activities beyond Merlin's wildest dreams. However, on the other hand, you have extremely dumb and monotonous machines that require extremely detailed instructions to perform whatever task you might have for them. And to make matters worse, they don't even speak your language!

What to do? Clearly, there needs to be someone, a person who understands both human language and machine gibberish, one who can translate whatever simple instruction you need to machine lingo and get them to perform whatever task we want. If only we could get someone who was smart, creative and knew his way around computers....

Dim the light, cue the music, and fix a smile on your face.

This is where you come in.

So What is Coding?

Coding, or computer programming, is the act of designing or creating an executable computer program to accomplish a specific goal.

In simpler terms, coding can be defined as the basic act (or should I say, art) of writing executable instructions for your computer in a language it can understand.

Remember the analogy above of extremely powerful by extremely dense aliens who need specific instructions in their language to carry out select tasks?

That is exactly what your computer is, and what coding, or more accurately computer programming consists of the art of writing said instructions in its own language or something close to it (actually no, but more on that later).

The act of computer coding itself involves processes such as analysis, creating, profiling and implementation of algorithms for a chosen programming language, amongst other tasks. While this may sound unbelievably tedious, relax. It really isn't.

These written instructions and directions you write for the computer to execute for you are called programs, which is probably why the term programmer describes someone who writes these instructions.

Now, coding sounds incredibly straightforward, doesn't it? You write your instructions using a certain programming language and the computer then immediately understands and carries out your process. Sounds about right, right?

Wrong.

The truth is, while coding is, as stated, the process of instructing computers, said instructions aren't actually written in the machine's language.

Let's go back to our alien analogy again. Here we have different civilizations whose language is fundamentally different from ours in almost every aspect imaginable. We want to communicate with them because they hold brimming stores of potential, and we're just bursting to unlock the stores of goodies talking to them will surely bring. There's only one problem - we can't.

So what to do? On a surface level, this problem seems intractable.

Until someone puts on the big brain cap and Sherlock Holmes arrives on the scene and notices something. Both us and the alien make and can understand memes.

Upon this amazing discovery, curiosity is ignited, a thread of commonality is established, and we and this alien force can finally communicate and get down to business. Through memeing.

Hey, stranger things have happened.

Hyperbole aside, this is a pretty good description for what happens when we actually use a programming language

Computers are simple basic machines that cannot grasp the human language. In fact, in reality, computers are really just a glorified bunch of circuits and transistor switches that understand just two things. A computer can only comprehend two different kinds of data - 1 (on) and 0 (off).

It is on this simple basis that practically all modern smartphone, tablet and laptop operation rests on, from watching a movie to winning at World of Warcraft. Playing a game, watching a movie, hosting a live stream with your webcam— all of it simply has to do with the opening and closing of transistor switches. It is nothing more than a unique combination of different transistor state types.

The mathematical description and representation of this on and off state of transistor switches in a computer is usually done with the Binary code, using 1s and 0s, with a number or digit each representing a transistor.

Binary code is arranged into bytes, which consists of 8 digits, each representing a transistor, i.e., 10001111 is one byte. 1100001111000111 is two bytes, and on and on and on. You can extrapolate just how many ones and zeros are contained in one kilobyte, megabyte, and gigabyte! The sheer amount of numbers there would make even the most neurotic numberphile swoon.

Every single 21st-century computer comprises hundreds of millions and billions of transistors switches, making the permutation of transistor switch combinations almost stretching to infinity. This is all nice and all, but there is a huge problem here - this is the only thing computers understand.

Computers respond only to binary switches and for any instructions to be carried out, it would have to be written in that language.

However, typing out these combinations in a series of 1's and 0's as it requires will take not only the patience of Job but literally your entire life before you got even 1% of whatever instruction was given.

Clearly, this was unsustainable, if only because they were a finite number of jobs (no relation to Steve).

So what to do? What could act as a bridge between these mindless series of zeros and ones and normal human language? That was when the brightest minds in the world came up with the idea of creating the programming languages that we love so much.

Simply put, a programming language is a bridge, an intermediary between our human language and machine binary speak. Programming languages are not the native language medium machines use for communication. Rather, they are the closest we can get to machine speak without spending half of our lives instructing a computer to shut down after we're done with it

Hence, in the interest of these machines carrying out our instructions as well as keeping our sanity, programming languages that were greatly similar to our native human tongues were invented.

However, they are much more hierarchical, structured and well organized and any instruction given must be completely logical without even the slightest margin of error for it to work.

Types of Programming Languages

Programming languages have many classifications and types, but they are generally grouped into two kinds - high-level and low-level languages.

High-level programming languages, as the name suggests, are programming languages more suited and designed for human use and abuse, in the realm of "high-level" cognitive humans. In contrast, low-level or assembly languages are the ones used for machine speak.

However, there still exists a problem.

While a high-level language is more suited to humans, it is automatically not suitable for computers.

Hence, to make such language understandable to machines, we will need a medium to translate our high-level chatter to machine speak. This medium is known as a translator.

What are Translators?

A translator, in computer-speak, is a medium that translates, or converts a code written in a certain high-level programming language, also known as source code into machine gibberish, called binary or object code.

There are different kinds of translators, namely

- Interpreters

- Compilers

- Hybrids

In computer programming, an interpreter is a translator software used to transform high-level programming languages to low-level machine binary.

An interpreter works by first processing the source code from the high-level language word for worrying, line by line, and converts the source code to machine speak one word at a time. In other words, an interpreter translation immediately starts running the moment code is input. It continues to do so until the end or it is faced with an error, such as an improperly transcribed piece of code.

Using this method, an interpreter detects errors very quickly unlike other translators and stops to report it. It is also much faster and starts performing the program immediately upon reading the code.

Due to its thoroughness, it is often employed as a debugging software as it scans through the source code one line at a time. It is also an easily movable language, as it does not depend on the strength of the processors.

A great example of an interpreted programming language is Python

Compilers

Just like the interpreter listed above, a compiler can also be employed in the conversion of a high-level programming language to a low-level programming one.

It carries out its operation burst, first converting the whole program to its own machine language in one session. Then, it reports back errors of syntax and improper coding detected during the conversion.

These errors also routinely interrupt the continuation of the compilation procedure, ensuring the program is not executed as no binary is translated.

A compiler is a very tasking language, as it does not generate machine language immediately, and is very processor dependent.

However, it is much more in-depth in scanning errors than any other translator.

Hybrid Translators

A hybrid translator, just as the name implies, is a fusion of both the Interpreter and the compiler translators.

It works first by compiling your high-level language source code into its own intermediary format, known in the case of Java as Bytecode.

This is then slowly and painstakingly interpreted by an interpreter, which immediately executes the program and stops when it detects errors.

The mix of these two is a very powerful and very useful programming language feature.

Assemblers

Finally, the last type of translator is the assembler.

Like its name suggests, an assembler translates assembly language to machine code binary.

Assembly language in itself is the lowest level programming language there is.

It is highly specific, depends on the architecture of the computer, and is the closest programming language to machine binary there is. It is also known as a symbolic machine code.

What an assembler does is that it translates this low-level language directly into machine code and feeds it to the GPU where it is immediately understood and instructions are carried out. Unless you're truly interested in specializing in computer programming, or drastically bored, you will probably never come across or use assembly language or its translator.

Why Should I Learn Coding?

If you're reading this book, you probably don't need much convincing on the advantages of learning programming.

But on the off chance you randomly opened this book or you're on a car trip on a journey to nowhere and you're stuck with this (not) boring book on coding, let me briefly highlight the importance of coding is and why it's the next big best thing after sliced bread, and why you should learn it as well.

1. Coding is fun

Look, a fundamental reason why anyone would want to learn something is pretty much because of how enjoyably challenging learning the concept is. It's pretty much why we can grasp social media apps quickly, but tax insurance forms seem like high school calculus. Passion determines interest. And interest determines your speed of learning. Learning is much faster when something is fun

And the art of computer coding is one such example which is fun, when learned properly, at the beginning at least, especially if you're the type that loves to explore and discover new concepts yourself.

The art of programming is, in many ways, an unfamiliar but highly interesting and rewarding landscape. It's like an Englishman trying to learn a new language like German, even more so in this case as you are literally learning a new way of speaking to nonconscious machines.

If you're someone interested in figuring things out for themselves or solving processes sequentially and logically, then you'd find coding a stairway to heaven.

And even if you're not, it's always fun to try out something new. Isn't it?

2. It pays, literally

Learning to code pays a lot, both educationally and finance wise. Coding and computer software development remain one of the most in-demand skills in the modern world. It has perhaps the largest job to worker deficit in current workplace history. In the USA alone, for example, there is a projection for as many as 2 million coders in the workspace!

This might sound like a fantastic over-exaggeration, but it really isn't. One of the reasons why coders are so in demand this modern technological age is that it *is* the technological age. The age of automation is almost fully upon us and while that might mean bad news to some, it's a boon to others.

If you're looking for a high-income skill with a massive earning potential, then computer programming is definitely a route to consider. Programmers earn fees up to 400k dollars a year, although of course it goes without saying you need a ton of experience before you charge such fees.

Even more promising, coding is one of the few available high-income skills with extremely high freelancing fees. Professional coders with a bit of experience under their belt can charge as high as 100 dollars per hour when working on projects for clients. It goes without saying of course that these are not your "run-of-the-mill" shed projects. But the massive earning potential is there, and with the rise of automation and computer integration into almost every sector of human endeavor, it's only going to get higher.

3. It helps you get the girls. Or boys.

Consider the following situation - A young attractive individual moves to your apartment block. They are young, friendly, and basically everything you've ever dreamed of. You want to walk up to them and take care of business, but you just can't get over your fear they wouldn't want you near them. You keep searching for an opening, but like the French imagined the Maginot Wall before the Second Great War, there is none.

Until, of course, fate smiles on you. This person's laptop suddenly displays a nasty streak of black and white code in the middle of the night while she's working on her life or death presentation. Stranded, desperate and in need of help, they cast their nets wide for who they can find to help them. Like the Bulls and mediocrity after '93, fate pulls her to your doorstep, you the techie guy with the mysterious magic know-how, who knows how to make broken motherboards sing. You meet each other, smile, and the sultry background music does the rest. Curtains closed.

Okay, while the scene I just described was pulled out a generic Philippine sitcom and might just be in the region of *"Never gonna happen"*, one thing coding **does** do is that it boosts your self-confidence and bank account enormously. And that is pretty much a people magnet. It also goes without saying that the societal imaging of coders has pretty much done a 360-degree flip (greatly aided by the rags turned riches success of the tech empire of course) from poor, socially awkward and maladjusted nerds, to rich, mysterious nerds. People dig that. Why not grab the knowledge and join the latest circle of cool?

4. It is fulfilling

Finally, it might sound corny but the truth is, computer programming is perhaps one of the most fulfilling and incredibly wholesome experiences you can have. With coding, you can literally conceive an idea, a thought, outline the steps needed to create it and bring it to life. Nothing in life is more exhilarating than this, save birthing a child, and in some cases, an app is literally a brainchild.

With computer programming, you can solve pre-existing challenges, identify new opportunities and even refine existing solutions to the hassles of modern-day life, while earning heavy, *heavy* , bucks for yourself.

What other life skill gives you the chance to do this?

There are numerous other reasons why you should learn to code of course, but this book was not written to convince or persuade anyone on learning to code, but rather to educate one on the key concept of programming.

However, before we proceed, we must briefly highlight the categories of coders out there and what they primarily do. This will help greatly broaden your knowledge of job opportunities, and perhaps you can find one that tickles your fancy straight away! Let's dig in!

Types Of Coders

What Types Of Coders Are There?

To fully grasp the whole range of the coding universe, it is important to know the different kinds of coders out there and what they do. Each different type has different languages and skills that make them excel at what they do. Although a basic understanding of coding languages is needed no matter your skill set, each programming skill set demands special skills and a more robust understanding of some programming language more than others.

To summarize, the different kinds of coders are:

1. Front-End Developer

These are the most popular and most versatile types of coders. They are the ones who made the web as attractive and easy to navigate as it is. If the internet were a house and programmers are people responsible for its constructions, front end developers would be like the painters and interior décor designers who make the house livable and attractive.

With that analogy, let me now explain who front end developers are.

Front-end developers are the coders who create and build everything *visible* on a web page. From content arrangement to styling to the way images are placed and words are presented on a webpage, all this falls under the purview of front end developers. In short, they are the aesthetes of the coding space. The success or failure of a website to appeal to viewers depends a lot on how talented its front end developer is.

Front-end developing is carried out in different ways, depending on the talent and skill of the developer. Still, the programming languages usually involved in front end programming are HTML, CSS, and JavaScript.

The major tasks a front-end web developer is responsible for are:

- Conceptualizing the idea of a website design from scratch and turning it into reality by writing hundreds of specific coding instructions for it.

- Ensuring the website is attractive, well-structured and organized and has an outlook pleasant enough to continue capturing user's interest. This can be done in a variety of ways, depending on the developer's creativity and the client's specification.

- Ensuring the website contains enough relevant keywords, has very fast responsiveness and does not "lag" while loading, and is not, in order to ensure it has a high search engine optimization (SEO) rating, which of course plays a major part in how many users will access the website.

Clearly, as is now quite obvious, front-end web developing is no small task as the developers involved are literally on the front lines of operations when it comes to the battlefield that is the internet.

However, on the plus side, front-end web developing is quite straightforward and very easy to understand.

Front end developers are also the most populous type of coders there is, so you'll probably have a lot of resource material and helpers along the way!

However, the downside to this is that it is the lowest-paid out of all coding jobs. If you're into coding primarily for money, you might want to consider some other option.

2. Back-End Developer

While front end Developers develop all the visible icons and interactive features you see on a website, a back end developer is the one who ensures the website or application actually runs and completes your task.

To use a simple example, while reading this book, log on right now to www.google.com. You'll probably notice the fancy doodles commemorating whatever new thing the world is celebrating, the search box and a host of other interactive elements. That is the work of the front end developer.

Now you can type in whatever you want and a moment after you hit the Google search button, it brings out results pertaining to what you type in. We've all used Google search before. We know how the process goes. It is like magic, right?

Wrong.

What actually happens, is that the moment you click "enter" on the box for your search inquiry, your local web browser sends a request to the Google servers for all information pertaining to your inquiry.

This request is then processed by Google servers, who then search their database, and respond back with all permissible information they have on your subject, all ranked in decreasing order of similarity to your initial search inquiry. This request is then stored on Google's database for future purposes and references next time. It's actually a bit more complex than that, but this simple explanation would do for the purpose of this analogy.

And who designs these servers and databases your search inquiry is cross-checked against? Yep. You guessed it—a back end developer.

In simple lingo, a back-end developer is one who creates the structure, and database needed to ensure a website or application runs optimally

If we were to compare the web to a house, then back-end developers are the architects and construction builders who ensure the house is properly built and sturdy enough against attacks (yes, back-end developers ensure web security too)

A few of the other things done by back end web developers are

- Creating a log in and log out portal for websites that are account-based.

- Creating algorithms that match up friend suggestions and other profile building activities on Social Apps such as Instagram and Twitter.

- Designing user-based applications and features that can be overlaid on a website. A simple example of this is Google Maps.

- Maintaining the security of a website and preventing data breaches and external attacks from malicious hackers

As you can see, back-end developing is a whole other and much more intensive ball game.

It requires an in-depth and solid understanding of a whole new different set of programming languages as compared to front end development.

The most commonly used language for Back-End Development include:

- SQL

- Ruby

- Python

- PHP

- And others, as needed.

Due to the intense nature of their job description and their extreme importance, back end developers are always in high demand. They are usually paid significantly more as compared to their peers.

3. Full-Stack Developer

Popularly considered the Jack of all trades, all-round coders, full-stack developers are pretty much the "one size fits all" coders for IT companies who cannot afford separate developer teams and want to build websites. As you can expect, becoming a Full stack developer means you must be well acquainted with both front end and back end languages such as HTML, CSS, Ruby, Python and the like.

Even though super proficiency is not a compulsory requirement, Full stack developers are usually still expected to be skilled enough in both front end and back end web development to get by. Full-stack developers usually act in a more managerial role, compared to other coder types

They are usually involved in the maintenance and troubleshooting of websites, and cross-checking website functionality.

4. Data Scientist

When it comes to programming, the data science field is like the new, cool transfer kid who drives an Aston martin and looks like Ryan Gosling.

Data scientists are one of the most sought after programmers today, as well as one of the highest-paid. It has consistently ranked high on top ten income-earning skills over the years.

But why the surrounding hype, you're probably wondering? Well, it's basically because of what they do.

Here's how data science works. Say, for example, you want to set up a manufacturing company right now. First you'd need to know just which commodity to produce, where to purchase the raw materials for your company, and which location is perfect for situating your manufacturing company.

You will also need to know the trade and distribution route, supply chain management and most optimal value stream for your goods. Finally, you need to be aware of the needs and quirks of your customers, which product they particularly like or dislike, and how effective your marketing strategy is. In short, you need information, and a ton of it.

Unfortunately, the information you seek is buried in a ton of individual data and disordered patches of knowledge that will probably make no sense to you. And that's where the data scientist comes in.

A data scientist is one that uses his mathematical knowledge of statistical analysis and data representation (both structured and unstructured), computer programming skills, domain skills and machine learning skills to "clean" and combines disparate pieces of data. They do this until they present meaningful information humans can draw insights from. For example, take the case of the manufacturing company. A data scientist will probably scour the web and tons of business reports and reviews, looking for the most profitable goods (after tax, of course) on average for a given amount of time. At the same time, and they eliminate other factors, which, as you can imagine, is insanely difficult on its own. Then they identify the most optimal production, distribution and retail routes for your products, and outline how best to market said goods. And this is greatly oversimplifying it.

As you can imagine, such dedicated research isn't easy. And it doesn't come cheap as well.

Data scientists employ programming languages like Python, SQL and Java to build algorithms and models to solve problems and optimize solutions, as needed.

5. Mobile App Developer

To briefly explain, a mobile app developer is one who, surprise, surprise develops apps for mobile phones, both iOS and Android.

As we are all aware, we are currently in the age of the smartphone. The demand for mobile apps has never been greater in history as it is now, making Mobile App developers very much in demand.

Being a mobile app developer isn't just a walk in the park, however. As different phones have different models, specifications and dimensions, it is the job of the app developer to write lines of codes for each operating system. This ensures the app operates on all platforms and doesn't crash or conflict with the inbuilt programs and restrictions on each smartphone.

Mobile app development is usually done using a programming language compatible with the operating system the app is being designed for.

Hence if you want to program iOS apps, you must be very proficient either in Swift or Objective C. Android programming on the other hand is done using Java, a very popular and easy to grasp language.

Mobile App development is also an extremely high paying profession and ranks as one of the top 5 income-earning skills today. The ball is in your court.

6. UI/UX DESIGNER

The great beauty and curse of the web are that it has no barrier limit, i.e., it is completely accessible to everyone. With a few clicks and tweaks and enough dedication, anyone can build a website, and people do. Millions of folks do. In fact, a survey done in 2020 holds that there are currently over 1 *billion* websites in existence! That's 1,000,000,000 websites for users of the web! Clearly there's a lot of competition. But say you want to make your webpage stand out above the rest, and you want people to fall in love with your website or web app immediately. How can you do such?

Simple answer - Hire a UI/UX designer

The user interface or User experience design is a special niche of computer programming that harks almost exclusively to aesthetics and satisfaction. If the internet were an art gallery, UI/UX designer would be painters who would make the art canvas of your website stand out vibrantly amongst others.

In more precise terms, UI/UX designers are technical artists solely responsible for improving the customer satisfaction for your site, usually done by tweaking the accessibility, usability, general outlook and page responsiveness amongst others for your website. They manage and brand your website in a way that is immensely pleasing to users.

A UX designer is also primarily responsible for embedding interactive elements like chat boxes on your website with the overall aim of maximizing customer comfort. UI/UX developers are mostly employed in-app rather than web design as it is where optimum user comfort is most desired.

Although coding is an integral part of what makes UI/UX designers, developers in that niche usually have an extra degree or in-depth experience in psychology and graphic design as well, to better understand what customers would like to experience. If you have a creative flair and love dealing with customer support and feedback, then UI/UX design is for you.

Coding VS Programming: The Difference

Throughout this book, you must have noticed that I have interchangeably used the word coding and programming at select times. If you are a relative greenhorn to the whole coding process, this might not mean much, but if you're a slightly experienced programmer with a more puritan taste, you must no doubt be livid by now. Very well, let us correct this misimpression.

Like almost all debates in life, the difference between coding and programming boils down to a matter of words, or more accurately, of perspectives.

Coding is, as defined above, the art of writing instructions in another language for a computer to execute, while programming is the art of identifying logical steps to solve a problem and writing machine instructions to execute said steps.

As you can see, both official definitions overlap, or more accurately, one role is subsumed into another. A coder is only concerned with writing precise unambiguous code for the machine to execute while the programmer is more interested in the bigger picture, of understanding what the instructions behind the code and how it will help solve whatever task is at hand. It is fairly accurate to say that coding is a subset of programming, and while all programmers are coders, not all coders are programmers.

In reality, it's pretty much just all semantics, a battle of words rather than a meaningful distinction. While coding *is* "merely" writing

31

code, coders to have to question the intent behind what code they are writing and how well it fits their purposes.

It's just like writing a letter to a loved one about an incident, say a burglary. The average person will probably write out how it happened and such straight away, but a novelist telling the event presumably will think about how well to structure the event to elicit maximum tension to keep readers glued to the pages and all.

Does this change the fact that they are both telling a story? Nope, one is just more interested in the overall structure of the plot than the other. The debate is far from settled, but that is essentially the difference between a coder and a programmer.

Chapter 2

Concepts Of Programming

In the preceding chapters of this book, we have clearly explained the definition of coding and how it basically works, outlined the difference between high-level and low-level programming games, and talked about the advantages of applying game-based learning to any learning concepts, including coding and computer programming. But what are the concepts of programming?

In this chapter, we will examine the four fundamental principles and features that govern every programming language. For the sake of this chapter, our chosen language will mostly be Java, a high-level language, but the same concept can be applied to any language. Consider it like the rules of penmanship. Once you learn how to write, you can express yourself in any language. But first, you must learn how to make pen strokes.

The concepts listed below are those "pen strokes" for writing computer instructions, in high-level programming languages. They are:

- Variables

- Control Structures

- Data Types

- Syntax

Variables

When you hear the term variable, no doubt the first thing that springs to mind is middle school algebra with its graphs and curves, and if you're particularly astute, some calculus. If you're a math whiz, or just generally awesome, you might remember this period with a fond smile and such. However, if you are like the rest of we humble 99%, remembering this god awful period of confusing dreary period of mathematical and learning confusion with dreadful shivers and scared programming will be more and more of that boring gauntlet of incomprehensible jargon, fear not. Relax. This isn't middle school math. And variables as a concept are really quite easy to grasp

So what are variables?

According to the Oxford Dictionary, the word variable means the ability for something to vary (don't you just love the helpful nature of dictionaries!), that is, *the ability for something to change with time or a similar parameter.* The easiest way to explain variables is to ask a similar question - What is NOT a variable?

The answer - A constant.

Hence, a variable is the opposite of anything that remains perpetually constant. Simple as ABC.

This might seem like mere pedantry, but it is this very definition and concept of variables that the bulk of every programming operation executed by a computer rests on. Hence every programming language has the concept of variable operations and parameters in its syntax (more on that later).

However, in coding lingo, the definition of a variable is a bit more streamlined than the general dictionary description. A variable is officially described as a unit or location of storage, or/and a symbol with an associated name that holds a known or unknown specific quantity of information, data or value.

Eyes glazing over? Knuckles tight with despair and boredom? Relax. Let me explain further. What the above word soup simply means is that a variable is merely a placeholder, a container of sorts that is used to save dynamic information for future use. To retrieve this saved data, all we need to do is to input this particular word or symbol. Consider variables the computer equivalent of voice recorders where you can tape your thoughts and play it back later when you've forgotten what you said and want to remember.

To use a much more practical example, let's use a real-life scenario you can encounter as a developer. For instance, you want to design a website for shoes and footwear company named yourshoes.com. Now, say the first thing either you or your client want to do is ensure you have the required shoe size for this prospective customer in order to save time on both ends. The first order of business then for you as a coder would be to assign a parameter that can measure your required shoe size against our available list of shoes, i.e., a *variable*. The best way for me to do this would be to build a textbox, probably named 'yourShoeSize', which is simply a symbolic store holder (the textbox that is), for your variable (your shoe size).

Hence, when a customer comes and types his/her/their shoe size, the program can then interpret it, compare it with the available shoe sizes present on the database and give you your required result.

This is a massive oversimplification, of course, but that's basically how variables work.

To use a much easier example, let us say, for example, you own a blog and you think it would be quite nice to send personalized email or newsletters to your customers' inbox. To do that, you would design a nice attractive textbox or pop-up on the screen, telling you to input your email in the chatbox below. The textbox below there is the variable. Why? Because it is the unit that acts as a store-holder for different sorts of information, in this case, emails!

The proper coding instructions of it would be as such - the textbox where you write your email will be termed 'yourEmail', this is the symbolic term for the variable data inputted in it (different emails).

Hence, when people go to your blog, like what they see, and subscribe for more content via email, their respective addresses will be stored in your assigned variable 'yourEmail'. Hence, when you, the owner of the blog now finally comes at the end of the day and asks "what value does the variable "yourEmail" hold?", the program would relay all the emails typed into that textbox! That, in a nutshell, is how variables operate.

Deceptively simple as it seems, this concept of variable is immensely important in programming and is the lynchpin a lot of coding operations are carried out. It's the use of variables that allows the concept of comment sections on social messaging apps such as Facebook, Twitter and Instagram to exist. It's what make you able to select what you want to get in online retail stores like Amazon and eBay. It's what makes your electric and gas bill payment work.... The applications of variables in computer programming is endless. As one programmer expertly noted, Variables *make the programming world go 'round.*

Now, just as different pens have different grading, color and tons of other minutiae specifications, different programming language has different variable types.

For example, we will be looking at the different kinds of variables in Java, an extremely important and immensely popular programming language. Learning how to code in Java is a requirement for many software development companies, and one of the games recommended in this book, the first one in fact, is sure to teach you how to code using Java, but more on that later.

Now, back to the subject matter of variables in Java, they are different datatypes as stated above that you would use in inputting those values, namely:

- String

- Integer

- Float or Double

What are these three ominously sounding terms and what does it mean, you wonder? Well, even better than telling you about them, let us use a real-life example to show you how they work.

Imagine you were asked to design a website for an investment company specializing in buying and investing in securities for people looking to have a fallback upon when they retire. To sign up on the website platform, they would have to input some personal details, such as their name, age, sex and how much their annual income amounts to. If you were coding such an app in Java, these data types would be stored respectively as

String : name

Integer : Age

Double : Annual Income

Your next question immediately of course is, why? And the question probably after that is....*why?*

I'm glad you asked.

This particular specification is peculiar and not universal. That is, it has to do with the nature of Java itself, rather than it being a general feature of all programming languages. And why is that? This is because Java is a strongly typed language, as opposed to being a weak one.

What does this mean? There are abstract definitions long enough to fill textbooks (and they do), but the largely simplistic definition is that strongly typed languages are programming languages that demand to know the specification of all data types being stored as opposed to weakly typed ones who allow for more flexibility. To use an analogy, strongly typed languages like Java is that parent who wants to know what you're going to do on a dinner date minute by minute while weakly typed ones are alright with you saying "we're going to have a great time"!

Both strongly and weakly typed programming languages have their advantages and demerits, and which is better than which is still being greatly debated by programmers and has no bearing to our current discussion. The reason for this slight detour is simply to highlight just why Java is the way it is.

As it is strongly typed, Java is a programming language that absolutely demands to know what type of information you plan to store in a variable beforehand. This allows the language to know with complete certainty only a certain "kind" of information is being stored in this variable and nothing else, just as you would expect your jar labeled "Salt" to contain only that and not sugar.

Hence, in our little scenario up there, variable types are specified before assigning symbols. Age is assigned the Integer type because, as the popular saying goes, *Age is just a number!*

As you probably recall in middle-grade mathematics, an integer is just a fancy way of saying *whole* number, with the emphasis on whole. Figures such as 4, 60, 300, 4359858855590884635003467 are all integers. The same holds for negative numbers, so figures such as -2, -49486, -48957385678593 and so on are all integers.

Integer data variable types must work for integers, whole numbers *only*. If, for instance, you input the value "12.01", you'd get an error message, even though it's basically *almost* the same as 12. But, like the anal lecturer you probably have met once in your education career, almost is not enough.

The same would happen if you inputted a foreign data type with the number. Inputting "$12" will similarly give an error message because the dollar sign is not an integer. For java, an Integer type variable stores only whole numbers and absolutely nothing else.

Similar thinking operates for the strings data type. Strings are data types used to , wait for it, *string* information together. Uncanny, right?

To be more serious though, string data types are variable data types employed to ensure that two different variables appear side by side, as though on a string. When used for sentences, sentences encoded with string data types appear just as two normal sentences, side by side, in the English language. To use a very simple example, the eponymous "Hello World" print program by Java consists of two variables and the string data type. In variable 1 we store the String "Hello", and in variable 2 we store the String "World".

The result? Well, hello, you know it. Hello World.

This precise specification of data types is useful in many ways. For one, the integer data type allows for the manipulation and mathematical operation of stored data in so many ways, meaning Java can (and is) employed in developing scientific and banking, finance and investment applications. Strongly typed languages such as FORTRAN and Java are most widely employed by the world's most foremost coders who develop software for investment firms and scientific practice for rigorous calculations. Assigning a type of data is an extremely useful application by Java that cannot be understated. In many ways, it determines how the data and operations with it will occur.

Let me use a simple illustration:

Imagine you are the back-end or full-stack developer for a retail e-commerce website. One of your jobs obviously would be to build a simple calculator that can add customer's goods as they select them. If you decide to go with, or are told to use Java to develop the site, one of your tasks would be to assign the variable integer, assuming of course, that all prices are whole numbers and they have no sign to prompt an error message, to the respective figures next to the respective prices of the goods so that the adding can be mathematically computational. Seems simple enough. And it is. Unless you make a mistake. And, alas, unfortunately, you do. (Before you flare up, relax. You *will* make a lot of mistakes in your coding journey. It is part of the learning process).

Your mistake this time is a very simple one. Instead of assigning the data type integer to the numbers, you assign another data type, say for example *strings* to them. What do you think will happen?

Normally, if your definition of the variables had been by the integer type, the operations would follow the normal rule of mathematics. For example, int 3 added to int 7 will result in the integer 10. As expected. Simple as ABC.

However, in this case, you have assigned the wrong data type to your variables. In this case, instead of integers, strings. So as you might have probably guessed, instead of simple addition and subtractions and other mathematical operations, customers clicking good items will see bizarre final bills indeed, and your client will definitely be less than happy.

For example, if you were to have two variables, 3 and 7 (just like above) assigned to strings, the result of adding these two variables together would be 37 instead of 10!

As you can see, the importance of data types cannot be overstated.

There are various types of data types for Java, (Boolean, final, char, float, etc.). Although they are much more advanced and in some cases complicated, they are all still essentially just place-holders or containers for assigning specific data types to different variables.

This basic concept of datatypes applies to all strongly typed languages, and the definition of variables apply to all programming languages, strongly or weakly typed.

This is one of the most fundamental concepts of programming.

Control Structures

The second fundamental concept of coding used in every programming language is a programming block known as Control Structures. Which sounds ominous and cool, doesn't it? It is. What does this block do, you wonder? The answer is very simple - it structures control (you should have seen that coming by now, eh?)

The official definition for control structure goes as follows:

Control structures may be described as a block of programming that analyzes variables and defines the direction they may proceed is based on certain pre-set parameters. The term flow control is used to describe the path direction executed by the program (i.e., which way the program flows). Therefore, flow control and command structures are the administrative decision-based body in computer programming, as the flow control determines the ultimate execution of the program based on certain parameters.

Well, well, well. All these sound rather hugely technical and immensely boring right now, don't they? Relax, they aren't. And like all basic concepts in programming, they are very easy to use once you get the hang of it.

So what are control structures? To use a more human example, let us consider a newspaper publication and their style of click-bait reporting to explain further. Say you are scrolling by your social media feed or walking beside the newspaper stand one day, not really interested and such until you see a huge attention-grabbing headline:

ATTENTION: ALIENS WEARING GREEN STOCKINGS AND BLUE T-SHIRTS LAND IN MANHATTAN!

> *Although it started out as a number, yesterday would no doubt remain etched forever in the minds of Manhattan citizens as one of the most shocking days in their history when Aliens with…… To read more, turn to page 63 (or in the case of a link, click here)*

Now, anyone confronted with this headline has a choice to make. If the headline sounds interesting enough to want to pursue further, no doubt you click the page link or buy the paper off the stand so you can flip to the said page. If, however, it fails to tickle your fancy, you dismiss it as another swirling pile of rubbish and proceed to rush to your job in Manhattan, where you are greeted by the shocking sight of Aliens wearing green stockings and blue t-shirts.

Tongue in cheek comment, aside, your decision at that time, (whether to buy the newspaper or click the link) is governed by a variety of factors, but most especially your curiosity. In a sense, the main parameter deciding whether to purchase or not hinged on how curious you were. Hence, this act of decision-making, the *flow* of command (to buy or not to buy) that proceeded after being confronted with a choice all depended on the news bait satisfying a certain parameter, i.e., your curiosity upon which the fulfillment (or not) of it led to two divergent paths. This is essentially what the control structures in computer programming is all about and how it works as well.

Here's how it works - when an executable program coded by you is running, what is actually happening is that your coded instruction, (translated to machine language) is being actively "read" by the said computer just like you'd read a book, (unless it's Arabic) - word for word, line by line, from left to right and top to bottom. This mode of machine reading is described as the "code flow" and it is what makes the execution of programmed instruction possible in real time.

But say there is a slight complication. Say there reaches a point where the program has different "options" to choose from in executing coded instructions based on whether certain variable parameters are fulfilled, such as your decision whether to buy a newspaper or not. The decision made can vary, based on the response. What happens then?

Well, just as you would choose to buy a newspaper depending on how curious you are, so would the computer "decide" what to do based on certain parameters. Of course, on a strict and already pre-set tableau of rules and guidelines to arbitrate where the direction of the program should run to if it faces such a decision (because, as you know, machines are very, very dumb). The computer could either choose to ignore the program, re-run it, or skip to another direction based on your guideline. It is this ability to effectively administrate and organize the list of available response for a computer in the face of shifting variable parameters that is known as a control structure.

Control structures are also a very fundamental concept of computer programming. They effectively determine the overall responsiveness and effectiveness of a computer program in the case of any eventuality. Like a general drawing up a contingency plan before a battle, control structures are what ensures your program still runs and is not caught flat-footed, even when shifting variable parameters are inputted.

Control structures are especially useful in game development, harking back to the early days of computer development, with the simplest games of chess being played. They are essentially what grants computer programs spontaneity and resilience, plus the ability to lay excellent traps, sniff out the dangerous move and lay those devastating checkmates you hate so much. Coded instructions such as "if he moves his king here, fork him with your knight" or "castle if, after the 5th move, he's brought his queen out" all mainly depend on control structures to be executed. So in a sense, you're not losing to a machine but nifty little programmers working through the bot. Feel good about never cracking "Advanced level" difficulty on your chess program yet?

So, we've established that control structures are basically just decision execution loopholes made by computer and triggered by dynamic variables. The immediate next question then is - what does it use to make this decisions and what triggers it to do so. Well, the answer to the latter is very simple - the difference in inputted variables, of course. The former is equally easy. Control structures use logic to make their decisions, of which there are three basic types, namely

1. Sequential Logic

This is otherwise known as the "default mode" for control structures. It simply specifies that the program should run line by line just as initially stated, unless given further instructions, i.e., sequentially. Sequential logic is the most simplistic command structure but is sometimes used in highly advanced programming modules to start an application, for example.

2. Conditional Logic

Now is where things start to get interesting. Conditional logic or selection flow, as it is called, is a slightly more complicated flow code in which the final output of the executing programming module depends on the presence (or absence), state and sometimes type of input variable supplied.

Conditional logic is a very popular control structure in different fields ranging from finance applications to game design. It is the backbone of many modern apps. This is because conditional or selection logic allows for specificity and branching purposes when making decisions, i.e., allowing for 2 or more different paths depending on the variable. Conditional logic has three popular types of selection statements to identify it namely

- The "if" statement

- The if/else statement

- The "if/else/if" or "Switch" statement

There will be more on this control structure later. For now, let us move to the third and final type of control structure there is in programming.

3. Iteration Flow or Repetitive Logic

This particular command structure is used to repeat lines of code over and over in a process called looping. In strongly typed programming languages such as C++, there are three kinds of loops namely;

- The "while" loop

- The "do/while" loop, and

- The "for" loop

Before we go into a detailed description and in-depth details for some of the control structures presented up there, let us take a look at one control structure statement and how it works.

Let us again use a real-life scenario. Say you are hired by a fitness and weight-loss company. They want to develop an automated weighing scale to automatically calculate the BMI of people who use them and determine if they are in a healthy weight range or not. That way, instead of merely measuring your weight and forcing you to do a clunky conversion, and then comparing it to the known standards to determine if you're overweight or not, the new weighing meter does it all for you. Just input your height, stand on its scale, and voila! It tells you if you're overweight or not. As the application of this software is largely conditional (i.e., different people have different weights), the control structure for the weight detection software will (probably) have an "if/else" statement that looks like this

```
if (yourBMI < 25 && yourBMI> 18.5)

{

// you are perfectly normal

}

else

{

// you are NOT healthy!

}
```

What is this inelegant chunk of clunky statements and what does it mean, you wonder? Well, this is what it means.

First, let us examine the variable(s) we have above - your BMI, short for body mass index. The program here is automatically comparing your particular result to the given BMI range to see if you fall in or not. If you are greater than 18.5 AND less than 25, you are in the green zone - healthy (because this is the value we assigned to it). But what happens if you're not in the given range? The opposite occurs.

The command this control structure is dictating is essentially this - if your BMI after standing on the weighing scale is in the range of 18.5 to 25, the first part of the code (you are healthy!) will be displayed and the instructions of the second segment are ignored.

However, if your BMI happens to lie outside both ranges (whether up or down), the program ignores the first segment and immediately proceeds to execute what is written in the second one, i.e., display you are NOT healthy. Sounds cool, right? And it is, really.

It is this act of designing multiple paths that allows the program to "choose" whatever option according to the input variable on the ground that serves as the foundational lynchpin for many video games and simulation software. There are other variations of the if/else structure, of course (and it will be further explained below, but this is basically how it works).

Another great example of a control structure that is very commonly used in computer coding is the while loop control structure. Here is how it works

if (yourBMI < 18.5)

{

  // you are seriously underweight

  // so keep filling up!

}

Or

if (yourBMI > 25)

{

  // whoa, you're a bit too big there fella

  // you need to shed a little, buddy!

}

What does this mean?

Well, let us stretch our BMI example a little bit. Imagine you wanted to specify the software a little further, so that it could tell users just which side of the divide they stood on the weight, i.e., whether overweight or underweight, because, well, people need to know!

There are a variety of ways a programmer can tackle this, but one of the most popular options to solve such an issue, of course, would be to make use of the while loop. This is a flowcode control structure whose singular purpose is to continuously execute the stated code between those two curly braces { } over and over and over until the condition fails to be met, or more accurately is false, will come in very handy.

The next question then is, what is then the condition? In this case, the condition is defined as whatever value is automatically inputted between the round brackets ( ), which is immediately contrasted with the standard BMI, of 18.5 or 25.

Hence, if you are less than 18.5 or more than 25, the executable program there will continuously execute the coded instructions inside those curly braces { }, i.e., display the underweight or overweight response.

However, the question that then beckons obviously is what happens when you fulfill those conditions, i.e., when you're over 18.5 and less than 25 in the Body Mass Index rating? Well, then the conditions become false (more on that later), and the code flow would not be executed at all when the computer reaches that section of the program!

It will simply skip that segment of the code and continue executing other sections of the written program below the loop structure.

Pretty neat, isn't it?

With those two practical examples in place, let us now discuss control structures in a little bit more detail.

Another construct that determines the flow of code in a program is known as the function construct, but the definition of that would be drifting too far from our current discussion. Suffice to say that the function construct is integral to the accurate execution of any flow code control structure.

True and False

As you might have noted in the examples used above, flow codes of selection and iterative statements greatly involve decision control steps. The activation of these steps all relies on fulfilling conditions. When these conditions are fulfilled, the state of the flowcode is true, and when not, it is called false, i.e., decision steps are summarily evaluated either as true or false.

This is an integral concept of flowcode structures and is used in every programming language. It is usually designed in strongly typed languages like C++ and Java as a Boolean data type (abbreviated as *bool*), which is only used to designate the variable true or false. It greatly improves the readability of the program.

True and false statements are also useful in identifying when to apply control structures and which to apply. Generally, in most cases, variables that define more than one situation or answer a yes or no question (such as the BMI case) will require a Boolean answer to properly execute the control structure.

Some languages automatically assume a Boolean condition, even without it being specified. For example, any C++ expression used to evaluate a value can automatically interpret a false or true condition as they present themselves. The golden rule is:

- Should an expression be evaluated to 0, then its truth value is automatically false

- Should an expression be evaluated to non-zero, its truth value is automatically true

Logical Operators

A key part of the operation of flow code relies on arithmetic, just like in mathematics. Yes, groan all you want, but basic arithmetic is an inescapable part of programming. Each programming language has its own slight modification to logical operators. Still, in this book, we will adopt the logical operators of C++, as it is very broad and easy to grasp. Also, basically every language adopts and uses the logic of C++ in their operations.

For C++, the arithmetic comparison operators employed are quite similar to the simple basic symbols employed in our normal mathematics. All of these operators return a Boolean answer - i.e., either true or false. Here is a list of all arithmetic operations permissible by C++

- a == b   // this operation means a is equal to b

- a!= b   // this operation means a is not equal to b

- a < b   // this operation means a is less than b

- a <= b   // this operation means a is less than or equal to b

- a > b   // this operation means a is greater than b

- a >= b   // this operation means a is greater than or equal to b

Now this sounds good, but what about cases like if/else statements where we need to combine expressions? Well, not to worry, C++ has got you covered with its Boolean operators. Here is a list of operations involving combined expressions.

- a && b   // this combines the operator AND with the operation which states that both a and b are true

- a || b   // this combines the OR operator and the operator which states that the operation is true if both or either a and b are true

- !b   // this combines the NOT operator, otherwise known as the negation operator and the operator which states that the operation is true if n is false

This combination of operators can be mildly confusing to grasp at first, especially in abstract but become much clearer when used in practice. They are basically what governs the test operators and their expressions of conditional statements and loop logic flow.

Here are some examples of expressions in control structures

- (a> 0 && b > 0 && c > 0)   // this expression means that all three variables a, b, c are positive integers, and that variable a is greater than 1.

- (a < 0 || b < 0 || c < 0)   // this basically just means that least one of the three variables (a, b, c) is negative

Control structures can also be expressed in different ways, and yet have the same meaning

(numBoys >= 13 && !(classPopulation > 70))

// this control structure means that there are least 13 boys in a class with a population that is at most 70.

Looks legit. However the code looks inelegant and confusing. It can be more simply expressed as

(numBoys >= 13 && classPopulation <= 70)

Which basically means the same as the expression above, only much more elegantly expressed. Writing clean, easy to read code is a highly prized asset in the programming world. It is always better to simplify things as much as possible.

Short Circuit Evaluation
When it comes to creating expressions, arrangement and thoughtful foresight are of the essence. This particularly comes to play when

considering a particular feature of && and || operators, known as short-circuit evaluation.

What does short circuit evaluation mean? Well, it's very simple, actually. It's simply an expression for something that immediately stops an evaluation when the leading variable has been found to be false. That's all.

To illustrate, consider a simple Boolean expression (A && B).

If A is found to be false, execution of the program stops immediately (i.e., short-circuits. Get it now) as there is no need to evaluate B, since, according to the Boolean expression, they are the same.

For example, consider the expression,

(a!= 0 && n / a > 0)

In this case, the short circuit is an absolutely integral one. Because if a is 0, an evaluation of n/d will result in an error message (i.e., illegal), which could affect your entire flowcode. So, the program reports false immediately upon the input of 0.

A similar move operates for the Boolean operation OR (||). Once the first segment of the expression is true, the program is immediately compiled by the compiler without scanning the rest as it is true by association. It must be.

The associative nature of this is a double-edged sword. It is hugely beneficial to some programmers as it allows them to write faster code with less compile time. However the massive drawback of it is that a simple poorly written instruction put first can throw a wrench and completely wreck your program. The choice is yours.

Now let us look further into Control Structure statements

Selection Statements
The if/else Selection Structure.

This is the most widely used conditional statement in programming. It's basic syntax comprises

if (input condition)

    statement

else

    statement

For languages like C++, the decision to add the else sentence is completely optional, as it can also be written in this format.

if (input condition)

    statement

The condition input in C++ is any expression that evaluates a variable value condition, otherwise known as R-value, and it must be enclosed in round brackets or parentheses ( ), as a rule for it to function. More of that will be discussed under syntaxes later.

The most common and easiest application of a selection control statement is to make the statement a Boolean expression, i.e., an operation which automatically evaluates a variable condition to be either true or false.

As said earlier, some expressions automatically have expressions that are automatically evaluated.

E.g., For a mathematical operation, any expression that evaluates to zero is automatically considered false, while any non-zero evaluation is true.

After the if and else words come the statement parts, or condition. They are in a sense the main body content of the if/else clause statements. There are different kinds of statements after the if or else words, namely:

- A null or "empty" statement condition;

- A one-line or single statement condition

- An expression; either single or combined

- A block of statement conditions, i.e., a compound statement, which can include multiple command conditions and single statement ones. They are usually enclosed with set braces { }.

It is common practice to indent (i.e., leave a little distance) between the if clause and else clause statements and the main body content of the executable program, as this greatly improves human readability but in reality doesn't matter to the compiler. However, it will help you write clean code and could ultimately help you debug faster so it is advisable to do so.

Here are some other examples of if/else statements being mathematically applied.

Imagine you are writing a simple program to evaluate student's scores and separate those who passed from those who didn't, for further learning. Your command structure would look like

if (StudentScore >= 50)

   cout << "Ignore";

This is a very simple control statement. As you might have noted, there is no else clause here. This is because you're only looking for those who scored below the Student Score pass mark of 50 and nothing else. This code is simple, clean and works very fast, which is the holy grail of computer programming.

What if, however, you want to do the reverse? Say you want to identify the really brilliant students in the class, those who scored well above the A grade for honor roll. A control structure to execute such a command will probably look like this:

if (StudentScore <= 70)

   cout << "Ignore";

else

cout << "There is a value";

This command structure, which is a combination of single statements is equally solid and simple as well. It tells the program to ignore every score below 70 and only execute the else clause segment when a score above 70 is discovered. Simple and neat, yes?

```
if (a!= 4)

{

    cout << "Wrong number";

    a = a * 2;

    counter++;

}

else

{

    cout << "That's it!";

    success = 1;

}
```

What does this mean to you? By now, you should be able to understand that the program is executable only when a is not equal to 4 and thus any condition that makes an equal to 4 will be countered, i.e., proven false. This is an example of a multiple statement expression, and it is the foundation of many complex programming modules.

Multiple statement conditions usually include a Boolean expression in them, i.e., true or false. This is absolutely necessary for the execution of the program as it directs the flowcode of the command structure, since one expression being true automatically means the rest are false and vice versa.

There are numerous other examples of if/else expressions and statements, but they all follow these basic principles. When it gets down to it, command structures are really fun and easy to grasp.

On a final note, be very wary of how you write and define your if and else clauses. An improper definition can lead to unintended consequences. For example, if you forget to use your curly brackets { }, you can include more parameters under a condition than you intend. More of this will be discussed under syntax.

The Switch Statement

Like the name implies, a switch statement acts just as that, a switch. It is a command structure often used on special occasions, where there are multiple options to select from. The syntax format for a switch statement goes as follows.

```
switch ( conditional expression)

{

    case constant:

        variable condition

    case constant:

        variable condition

    ... (as many case labels as you specify)

    default:        // optional label

        variable condition

}
```

This is how the switch statement works - first, it evaluates the variable condition, and then compares it to them and then compares it to the values in the case labels. If it finds a similarity between the two statements, the execution of that code immediately flows to that case label.

One of the requirements of switch statements is that the statements in the case labels must be constants, and can only be integer data types.

The Conditional Operator

There exists a unique kind of operator known as the conditional operator. It is known as such because it can be employed to write short coding instructions which execute themselves in a fashion similar to if and else clause conditional statements.

This is the Format for switch statements:

test_expression ? true_expression : false_expression

Here is how it works:

Upon running, test_expression is used to evaluate the true or false value for the variable condition stated. This is similar to how an if conditional statement works.

If the test expression is true, the operator runs the true_expression statement

If the test expression is false, the operator runs the false_expression statement.

Conditional operators are pretty advanced operator types. It is usually employed in the C++ language and is the only ternary operator for that language. A simple example for a conditional operator is this:

cout << (a > b ? "a is less than b" : "a is greater than or equal to b");

What this expression means is that the program should continue regardless of if a is greater than b, or is less than or equal to b. It can also be expressed using an if/else statement expression like:

if (a > b)

   cout << "a is greater than b";

else

   cout << "a is less than or equal to b"

There are other examples of control structures, but this will drift off too far further afield. Instead, I have chosen to limit ourselves to the easiest and most commonly used control structures employed for coding and computer programming today.

With those few control structures discussed, I believe you now understand what control structures are, and how they direct the flow of code, which is read like a book. We've learned we can manipulate the "flow" of code and execute segments of code repeatedly, without laboriously writing it over and over again.

Control structures are also an extremely important programming concept in programming, they are the backbone of what makes all web software and applications run and properly function. If variables are the lifeblood of programming, then control structures are the veins and arteries, which direct where the blood will flow to. Or more accurately, they are the "brain" of all coding, as they determine just where and how the flow code will work. Which do you reckon is more important? I'll leave you to it.

Data Structures

The third fundamental concept of coding we will discuss as regards coding games is one slightly more interesting than the previous one and relatively much easier to grasp the concept (thank God, eh), a concept known as data structures.

So what are data structures and what are they used for? You are about to find out.

Data structures, in computer science, can be simply defined as a particular mode or way of saving and arranging data on a computer for more efficient use. Simple as ABC.

Alright, let's get more technical. What does "more efficient use" mean? To illustrate the meaning of this and how it can be applied, let us consider a real-life practical scenario (you know how much I love those!) where data structures can be applied.

Imagine, if you will, that you're interning in the data processing division of a software company and one of the tasks assigned to you is to organize and itemize the contact numbers of every single worker in the company (if that sounds depressingly boring to you, remember some people actually do this, *as a job)*. Needless to say, there are quite a list of numbers to store! Even more, this contact list is not constant, as it could expand or shrink at any given time depending on employment vacancies and workplace reshuffling. Now the smart thing to do of course is to automate this dreary job, so you do, and good job! But then, what next?

Normally, your line of thought, with the level of knowledge you have right now, would be to assign these numbers as variables in an executable program. You will build an if/else command structure to ensure "old" workers, (i.e., workers who leave the company) are not mistakenly included in the official company's contact list when it's time to refresh the list.

Say, for example, the number of workers in the company is 10 (play along with it), you would simply assign 10 string variables and get along with it right?

Something like,

String worker1, worker2, worker3, worker4, worker5, worker6, worker7, worker8, worker9, worker10;

worker1 = "CEO, James Bond (james.bond@someCompany.com)";

worker2 = "Susan Parks (susan.parks@someCompany.com)";

worker3 = " Floyd Mayweather (flood.mayweather@someCompany.com)";

and on and on till you reach worker 10. Looks legit, right?

Well, yes, but no.

See, one of the most valued traits of programming is efficiency and minimalism and ease of execution. And the code written up there literally tanks in all these listed sectors. The program up there is undesirable mainly because of two reasons, and no, James bond being CEO on the list is neither of them.

The prodigious amount of text characters you will need to write your program so it can work. Of course, with just 10 contacts, it doesn't seem that stressful but imagine if this were a *real-life* scenario and the said company has 300 workers, each with two different contacts, one a home number and the other mobile. That involves specifying the variable for each contact, over six hundred, 600, of them!

That is nothing other than sheer torture! No one deserves to go through that kind of horror.

The extremely inflexible nature of the program.

Typing out the program like this would mean it is impossible to add new contacts every time without first manually re-editing the program. That means *every single time* you want to add or remove new contacts from the program, you will need to rewrite the program all over again. And that is simply mind-bogglingly sad.

All these rants above can be simply surmised into one simple statement - writing code in that way is *inefficient*. Clearly there must be a better way to code these statements then, you might then wonder. And in that you are absolutely right. There IS a better way to develop a program suited to this challenge and efficiently maximizing data output with minimal input work.

So, what is this better way we speak of? You guessed it - data structures.

Before we delve into what data structures are and how they work, let us take a look back at our contact saving exercise once again.

One noticeable feature about this contact data is that they can be arranged serially or sequentially, with one number coming after the number on and on and on, in annotated form, i.e., just like a list!

Another noticeable feature is that these contacts all contain the same data type, i.e., integers, because they are phone numbers and phone numbers are, well, *numbers*.

Combining these two threads of commonality together, one must wonder; isn't it probable to build some kind of element that can let you organize these variables more efficiently? The answer is, yes you can! And these elements are called data structures.

In the above examples, the phone numbers can all be organized under a data structure called Arrays, and a sequential arrangement of the data is possible using a data structure called a List.

If these two data structures are combined, here's how the code program is going to look like in Java:

List contacts = new ArrayList();

Whew. That looks much more immensely neater and accessible, doesn't it?

"Ok, yeah, sure, sure, but what does it do" you may be wondering. Well, for one, it makes the whole adding and removal of contacts from your list much easier. How so, you wonder? Well, for one, instead of manually assigning and designating new contacts, what is done is new contacts are added to the *data structure* rather than being assigned a variable of their own! It resembles something like this:

contacts.add("CEO, James Bond
(james.bond@someCompany.com");

contacts.add("Susan Parks (susan.parks@someCompany.com)");

And that's all! Like magic, it gets added to the list.

"Uh, ok. So what's the difference between this and the former one" you might be wondering. Well asked. On the surface, the difference is not much, they both involve inputting data, but the main difference is *how* these data types are assigned. Unlike the previous one where you had to create a specific variable for each contact number on the list, this second approach involves you creating just one variable, which is (contacts). The importance of this is immense, especially when it comes to adding and removing new contacts. Instead of manually always creating a new variable every time you want to add a new number, all you need to do each time you want to create one now is type contacts.add(someRandomContact), greatly improving the flexibility and dynamic applications of the code.

Similarly, deleting contacts will not require manual re-editing of the entire program every time, but simply the manipulation of the specific data structure. This is the true power of data structures - it grants you the ability to manipulate your code as dynamically as possible in response to current challenges without rewriting the whole thing all over again manually.

In essence, a data structure is a structure that lets us get around the hassles of having to define lots of variables in our code.

There are different types of data structures for different programming languages. However there generally exists these three types:

- Array

- List

- HashMap

And so on.

We've talked about the first two on the list, so let's briefly touch on HashMaps.

What are Hash Maps? How best to highlight their functions than to, as I always love to do, first see how they are applied. Imagine you are an experienced full stack developer called in to troubleshoot a retail e-commerce website which has been having some problems with bugs and such. The first you do of course is to run the software on your IDE (more on that later). Upon running the code, you begin noticing some arrangements such as:

"Shoes" -> "Oxfords", "Brogues"

"Utensils" -> "Spoons", "Forks", "Knives"

"Knives" -> "Japanese", "Western"

"Shirts" -> "formal", "casual"

If you see something like that, don't be afraid. And it's not the problem (unless it is).

Let's take a further look at this highlighted example.

One thing you notice here is that there are "general" names of items on the left, which point to more specific ones on the right. This pairing up of values is in the coding circle as a Key/Value pair.

The "key" in these instances are the general items - shoes, shirts and such, and value here means the specific items from the general list.

This pairing arrangement is possible due to a HashMap data structure! This is a very useful concept that is applied to almost every retail website! For example, if you want to buy something on Amazon right now. Let's say a phone. Where does the home page of the website first take you? To the electronics section! Next, you choose the phone maker, (also making use of a hash map), where you fill your specifications and such. This similar application of

HashMap has tremendous potentials in our manipulation and application of data variables.

While the representation of HashMaps I gave up there looks rather fancy, the truth is, HashMaps are slightly more complex than that.

For example, here's how the HashMap of the program I showed you would look like, in Java code.

```
Map<String, List<String>> Shoes = new HashMap<String,
List<String>>();

shoes.put("Oxfords", new ArrayList(Arrays.asList("Brogues",
"Loafers", "Monkstraps")));
```

Whoa, right?

That's a lot of brackets. Let's break it down a bit.

As you know, the HashMap data structure is used to store key/value pairs. In this selected example, our key was shoes and the value pairs are the oxfords and such. Remember that the data type is a string. And because the collection of data is similar, they are defined by arrays. Now we get to an interesting part. Say a new type of shoes was just shipped in and we want to add this new option to our web app. What is to be done?

Traditionally, the "old" method would be to rewrite the code repeatedly, which is mindless drudgery and pretty much depressing.

Instead what we do is create a new list of Arrayed data, insert it in our HashMap, and voila, done!

This is made possible because a unique feature of data structures is that they can be nested, i.e., a data structure can be written and stored in another one. This is not an uncommon concept well-practiced in the coding world, i.e., putting one data structure inside another. This helps it fulfill what it was initially meant to - maximize the efficient organization and use of executable data without hassle.

Syntax

Now we move on to the second to the last, but certainly not the least most important concept in coding everyone has to master - syntax. In fact, it is the opposite of unimportant; having good syntax is a necessary prerequisite for every programmer. You can't call yourself a programmer if you don't know Syntax.

With that wonderful introduction, you're probably now wondering - what is this syntax you're talking about and how does it work?

Well, according to the dictionary definition, syntax is summarily defined as a term used in linguistics to refer to the pattern and fundamental principles that direct how words are combined to make up clauses, phrases and sentences. It simply means writing sentences of any language *in the right way.*

Well, that's rather simple isn't it? Surely the coding definition will be much harder. Well, hate to break it to you, but it isn't.

74

Syntax in computer programming is simply defined as a formal set of principles or rules or statements that govern how symbols are combined in programming languages to form correctly structured programs. Just as in the linguistic definition, computer syntax is concerned with you writing code the right way.

Alright, this sounds simple enough, and it is. Syntax is just how code is written. Take particular emphasis on the *"how symbols are combined"*. This is the major difference between linguistic syntax and the computer one. Unlike the normal definition of syntax, which concerns itself just with words, computer syntax encompasses all kinds of characters and symbols. Symbols such as ampersand, brackets, both round and curly, numbers, variables, asterisks, underscores and such are all part of what is governed by a language syntax. For example, when writing an email to someone, you have to input the email address it's being addressed to, which probably looks something like email.message@randommail.com, right?

When you click send, the program executing your instruction will read every single character in this email address as one distinct element. So, if for example, you forget to add a . or a @, you instantly get an error message, even though the words are complete. The same principle works in programming, and doubly so! If you do not use the proper syntax for the programming language you choose, your code might, nay, *will,* never run even if it is 100% logically sound! What a bummer.

Why are computers so anal about syntaxes, anyway? Why can't they just live and let live? Well, it's because they can't. Live, that is. Remember when we talked about how dumb computers are? Well, don't let the awesome concepts we've been mentioning so far fool you. Computers are still very dumb. So dumb they need everything spelled out for them. And so dumb they can't recognize the difference between word characters and symbols.

Just as every human language has its own rules of grammar peculiar to it, each programming language has its own special syntax, and what applies for one language does not apply for others. Similarly, what you can get away with in one language can bring back error messages in another. This is particularly true for the syntax of weakly typed language as compared to those of strongly typed ones.

For example, if you're looking to assign a variable in Java, your syntax will probably look something like this:

String newVariable = "Jesus Christ, this is cool!";

This is a legitimate code, simple and clean. Let's dig in a little at what is going on here.

Right up there, in that simple program, there are syntax segments that make up that variable. The first is the data type of the variable. Recall we talked about data types under variables and how strongly typed languages like java absolutely need to have the type of variable data specified before inputting it. As the variable in use consists of word characters and a symbol (!), not numbers, the String type variable is used. That is one part of the syntax.

The second segment of syntax parts is the name of the variable, i.e., the "newVariable". Variable names are simply tools that act as symbolic placeholders for the variable (as you are already aware of), and are made up of letters and numbers. Some can contain underscores, but that is the only symbol they can hold. Variable names by convention are started with a lower case letter, but that is mainly a conventional matter. It does not affect the code output in any way.

The third syntax area concerned in defining the variable above is the value the variable itself contains. Our example is that of a string variable, so it *must* contain only words and characters. String variables are slightly more forgiving, as compared to other variable data types. If, for example, the variable data type had been "integers", typing in words for such a data type will result in an error message.

Take special note of the quotes (" "). In Java, string types are defined by encapsulating regular symbols and letters inside quotes. This is simply one of Java syntax peculiarities. Other languages are more lenient.

Finally, the concluding part of the syntax for this variable was the semicolon (;) symbol, which marked the end of this code segment as complete.

In Java, the semi-colon character is used to indicate the end of a code. It is the programming equivalent of a full stop in our normal English language. Again, this is peculiar to Java; other programming languages have their own syntax ending. The semi-colon must be used. Without its placement, the code segment hasn't stopped, as far as your computer is concerned.

And there you have it, all the syntax segments for that simple code. What happens when one is missing? Well, as you can probably guess, the code won't run! If you fail to specify the correct data type for a variable, neglect to encapsulate the characters of a string with quotes or ignore to end the variable properly with a semi-colon, your code will generate an error message anytime you try to run it. So as you can see, the full package of syntax, proper character placement and all is extremely important in ensuring your code functions as it should.

Not all languages have such rigid requirements and strict syntax rules like Java, however. Some are much more permissible to loosely defined variables and have a greater degree of flexibility in their syntax. A classic example is Ruby and Python syntaxes.

Learning to write proper code syntax will probably be your greatest challenge as a beginner, but after you start to read and write a lot of code, you'll probably get used to it. Syntax remains however, a key concept of programming. You cannot call yourself a programmer and effectively code in a programming language without knowing its syntax.

Chapter 3

Coding Games

Before going too far in the book, it will do us well to mention the coding games we will be looking at to let the key coding concepts.

Without further ado, let's dive right in.

Robocode: What is Robocode?

Alright, let's begin by asking the big questions - What on earth could a game that has robots and code in its name be about?

Well, as it turns out, Robocode, disappointingly stays true to its name - it is a coding game whose main aim is about building a robot battle tank to do battle against other robot tanks, gladiator style. The true novel feature about this game however that differentiates it from a thousand generic video games out there is that *you do not actually participate in this game.* Instead, the only thing you'll be responsible for is programming instructions for your robot tank, thereby guiding it in the heat of the battle, which is obviously occurring in real-life. In a sense, it's more of a strategy game than an action one, where in this case, you're a supreme general directing your troops to battle, but ultimately unable to influence what happens on the front lines.

This falls in line with the Robocode motto which says *"Build the best and destroy the rest."*

Although Robocode is an instructive and exciting strategy game, what makes it truly unique and different from the rest is the fact that it is a programming game. It is an immense learning resource for anyone hoping to get familiar with the concept of coding and computer programming, especially the language in which Robocode uses to program robots, which is Java.

Nevertheless, Robocode is very useful in learning other high-level object-oriented programming languages as well, such as C#.

Robocode is so useful and important in learning to program that it is employed as a means of generally introducing students into Artificial Intelligence and programming by different learning institutions around the globe who have seen the light of game-based learning.

To be fair, Robocode sells and markets itself well; its basic concepts are quick to grasp. Despite its medium of creation, it still retains the fundamental attractions and perks all entertainment since ancient times have held - the thrill you get from blowing up enemy tanks is as comparable to a headshot in Call Of Duty, or checkmate in chess.

To make things easier and smoother for users, Robocode comes with its own executable programming implements already - namely an installer, AI editor, and translator (a Java compiler) which ensures the coding development environment is perfect.

Due to basic operating system requirements however, Robocode only runs on systems with a pre-installed JVM (Java Virtual Machine), you know, being that it's programmed in Java.

With that in mind, the game developers of Robocode have the foresight to include everything of particular importance in its main file.

Similar projects such as Eclipse and Visual Studio which also contain external IDE are in turn allowed to run in Robocode which is advantageous as they are much better for developers than Robocode's default editor.

As stated above, Robocode was built with Java. This means that it is able, and indeed only runs only operating systems already installed with Java.

This is not really a restriction, as almost every system today such as Windows, Mac OS, Linux and UNIX all have Java editors pre-installed.

To make the game run smoother, however, it requires the installation of Java 6 and some other specifications.

You know how these things go.

Several gamers and users of Robocode have reported that the game is very interesting and fun, but quite addictive.

The truly amazing thing about Robocode is that in this age of over-commercialized software and where almost every useful app always comes with cash purchases, using Robocode is free of charge!

This partly has to do with the fact that Robocode actually started as a side project and with the ideals of its developers who just genuinely want developers and others to sharpen their coding skills.

Talk about living Mother Teresa's in the age of silicon.

Another great feature of Robocode is that its code is available to everyone, i.e., an Open Source project, under the EPL (Eclipse Public License) term.

This basically means anyone can go on the net and view just how Robocode was coded. Yet another rare example of openness and trustworthiness in today's age.

History of Robocode

Like all great features such as Facebook and email that we enjoy today, Robocode was created in the early 2000s.

Inspiration for the game, however, goes back further than that. Its immediate precursor is widely regarded as Robot battle, (notice the similarity) , a game developed in 1992 by Brad Schick.

His game was in turn, also inspired by Robot War, a game accredited to Apple in the 1980s.

The Robots sure got a long history, don't they?

Robocode itself properly started as a pet peeve side project by Matthew A. Nelson, an amazingly talented programmer. After developing it, and possibly perhaps realizing how cool it was, he decided this game was too cool not to share, and he professionally introduced the game to IBM (yes, the IBM) under Alphaworks, in July 2001.

Often vilified (and rightly in some cases) for not being the quickest on the uptake, IBM quickly got the hint this time, perhaps envisioning even back then the future potential for the game.

Without wasting a moment, the mega-company immediately began massively Public Relations and hype for the new, much like the 2000's hype for the PlayStation Consoles and took to amazingly goofy lines such as *Rock 'em, sock 'em Robocode!* for publicity promotion.

Despairing cringe aside, the game managed to survive and escape a lifetime of perpetuity in nerd suburbia but instead rose to immense popularity upon its release, thanks to IBM aggressive publicity and its own innate attractiveness

As earlier said, it has withstood the test of time as has remained the number one resource for an introduction to programming and AI in schools around the globe.

After repeated urgings by its original programmer Nelson, Robocode was officially unfurled as an Open Source project by 2005. That however led to the discontinuation of Robocode development, because, well, no profits if it's all out there.

To bridge the gaping hole, fans and community forums already built around the game started developed their own versions and upgrades to the game, complete with malware fixes and updated features such as "Contributions for Open Source Robocode."

After much patient programming, two updated projects named RobocodeNG and Robocode 2006 were eventually created by Larsen Flemming

With that developed, Larsen asked for and was in time granted executive control over the open-source Robocode project at SourceForge, and became inaugurated as Code Administrator and official developer in 2006.

Due to incompatible features and a myriad of other reasons, RobocodeNG, one of the two upgrade contenders was finally dropped and Robocode2006 was eventually accepted into the official version with a host of improvements.

This in turn has spurred repeated and meaningful contributions to the game from several sectors lc the Robocode community, one of which was RoboRumble

Officially inducted in May 2007, RoboRumble was popularly received by the Robocode family, who immediately employed it in creating features such as Meelee, 1 v 1, as well as twin and group competitions.

Another momentous advancement that happened to the game came in May 2010 by Pavel Savara, an ardent member of the Robocode community.

His great contributed was that he provided a .NET plugin in May 2010, finally allowing a "bridge" so to speak between .NET/Java. This basically allowed for the creation of robots in programming languages different from Java, something that was impossible before.

However, for the purposes of this book, I will advise you to stick to its native Java language, unless you have already started another language or attained proficiency in it.

Computer Specifications

The list of things needed for the smooth operation of Robocode include:

- A Java 6 Standard Edition, SE, or the latest Java version

- The Java Developer Kit, JDK, or the Java Runtime Environment, JRE, can also be applied.

- There are also some important conditions and directory specifications that must be implemented before starting up Robocode. They include :

- JAVA_HOME should be set up to sync with the same directory for Java (JDK or JRE).

- Windows example: JAVA_HOME=C:\Program Files\Java\jdk1.6.0_41

- UNIX, Linux, Mac OS example: JAVA_HOME=/usr/local/jdk1.6.0_41

- PATH should also specify the directory path to the bin of the Java home (JAVA_HOME), a path that also includes java.exe for starting the Java Virtual Machine (JVM).

- Windows example: PATH=%PATH%;%JAVA_HOME%

- UNIX, Linux, Mac OS example: PATH=${PATH}:${JAVA_HOME}/bin

- The final system requirements specify that the plugin for the Robocode .NET APU should be installed right over the Robocode application in the case of those who wish to build their robots via .NET.

The installation of this plugin is just like the installation of the Robocode app itself, via a double click.

Getting Started

RoboWiki provides almost all the available information on Robocode. Apart from all the information about Robocode, RoboWiki also houses the Robocode community. You can check out

RoboWiki for any additional information you wish to learn about Robocode.

Getting Started

Before diving into the battle arena, you should first study the anatomy of a robot, understand the scoring system, know the game physics and so on.

Robot development is a never-ending activity on the Robocode platform, especially with the new inclusion of a .NET framework. Different articles exist online guiding people on how to develop their bots

1. ROBOCODE API

Robocode API is rather unique when contrasted with other games. Unlike any other robot game, the API is designed to display as an HTML page

Robocode is comprised of mainly three kinds of API.

Robot API: The first is the Robot API, the only segment containing a Java package and a .NET namespace.

Both packages are used in the development of the robot tanks.

Robot Interfaces: The second API bundle contains the very interface of the game itself.

They are the Java package robocode.robotinterfaces and .NET namespace Robocode.RobotInterfaces.

The Robot interfaces are responsible for the visual and graphic aspects of the game. They are also very involved during the creation and addition of a new type of Robot to the traditional Robot API. They are not however involved in changing the control and behavior of the robot. Only the traditional design and interface.

Control API: The third and final API package for Robocode is both the Java package robocode.control and .NET namespace Robocode.Control.

The Control API, in a way, is the very heart of the game itself. The control API is responsible for engaging in the actual art of kickstarting battles and assessing results from the battle arena.

2. Robocode Repository

One amazing thing about open-source projects is the innovative ability that comes with sheer creativity. A prime example is this - the Robocode repository.

If you are bored of the sample robots provided by the game, or you just generally want your robot tanks to look fiercer, there is a whole retinue of other robots in what is known as the Robocode Repository. The extra samples can be found in the Bots segment of the said repository.

The idea of a Robocode Repository is the brainchild of David Lynn, another gifted programmer who devised and maintained the repository as an independent addition to Robocode.

3. Community

As you no doubt already expect, the huge popularity of Robocode has similarly led to a devoted online fan base known as RoboWiki. Different strategies, ideas and, of course, rivalries are often discussed on the RoboWiki forum. It is also the official information outlet for Robocode upgrade as developers themselves are present on the same forum as well.

RoboWiki provides strategies such as:

Radar

Movement

Targeting

Code Snippets

4. Challenges

Without challenges, there can be no improvement. RoboWiki points out the famous challenges that are available for testing and studying the robot's movement, gun abilities and targeting. Those challenges are:

Movement Challenge

Targeting Challenge

RoboRumble Gun Challenge

5. Competition

The best way to challenge yourself as a robot developer and your developed robot is to go to RoboRumble@Home.

RoboRumble is just what its name suggests - a rumble of robots. It is a game exhibition annually organized by Robocoders to show each other who's boss.

RoboRumble is organized first by assessing the level of power availability present in the Robocoder's computer and uses it to spilled the strain of fighting battles and organizing your rankings.

The robot has three main sections:

- RoboRumble (aka 1v1): As the description suggests, the 1 v 1 method is a simple duel, mano a mano. It works by pitching one player robot against a fellow player. It's simple, clean, and may the best bot win.

- *Melee* Rumble: Just like a battlefield of foreign soldiers, melee rumbles consists of ten robots randomly selected and told to wage war against each other. The winner is determined by the last man, sorry, robot standing

- Team Rumbles: "Two heads are better than one", the adage goes. So how about five? Unlike previous rumbles, the team rumble is comprised of 2 main teams, each consisting of five robots told to fight against each other. The last team standing wins.

There are several websites and articles available online to assist you in your incredible journey to RoboRumble.

Other competitions which exist in the RoboRumble world are:

- Twin Duel: the twin duel pitch two teams against each other in a battlefield that is 800×800. Each team is made up of two robots, hence the name twins.

- Hat League: In this contest, a bit of pure probability is applied. It involves the purely random selection of two teams who have no idea of each other's talent or skill, hence the likening to picking from a hat. These two teams comprise two robots and like two strange generals meeting on the battlefield, they must combine strategies and plan how to defeat their two also randomly selected opponents. Let the games begin!

6. Command Line:

A special characteristic of Robocode is that you can choose whatever options and pre-defined property on how you want the game to go, even while it is running

A good example of how this command line operation works is by

- Uninstalling the graphic user interface (GUI) command for the game.

- Uninstalling the preinstalled security for Robocode. This however is limited to the game; the security for your system's JVM is not affected

- The ability to edit moves and battle strategies from an already pre-existing Robocode. battle file.

- Visually replaying a pre-recorded battle.

- Allowing the storage of battle results on a different comma-separated file

1. LINKS

Present in Robocode's home page is the important places to deepen your understanding of the game further.

Home Page of Robocode

The home pages of the RoboWiki contain directions and further links to different challenges in the Robocode universe.

7. Feature Requests

Ideas for new features and improvements are highly welcome and can be submitted as a feature request.

Developers with great ideas and the know-how of implementing them can go ahead and implemented the accepted features. The successful implementation of the nee feature by the developer automatically makes said developer a contributor of Robocode.

There are several sources that better explain how to better contribute to the development of Robocode. Implementations are accepted under the EPL terms.

8. Versions

Robocode is a never-finished product as there are constant changes and developments made. Currently, there are three different Robocode release types and they are:

The Alpha Version: as the name suggests, this is the first "draft" of the Robocode release type. They basically contain undeveloped features and new gameplay. They are usually distributed to select individuals and are not to be released to the public.

Beta Version: This is the name version we are all familiar with. Like the alpha Version, it contains the upgrade to Robocode with all malware fixed and new features. It is usually available for a small sample of the public to try out and get a feel for. Beta versions are usually released to a small but diverse pool of people whose feedbacks and recommendation are highly valued in making the final version.

Final Version: And the last, but certainly not least release type for Robocode is the final version, with all kinks and malware fixed, and exciting new features added. It is available to the general public without any restrictions or complaints.

9. News

Robocode has a dedicated blogspot where new and exciting updates about the game are released.

There are also Twitter and Facebook handles for Robocode to be followed to obtain timely information. There are also Twitter pages for RoboWiki and RoboRumble

10. How to Contribute

Contribution to Robocode can be something of a bother, as the game lacks proper documentation about its internal mechanics and working, as it has no codebase.

Due to the lack of a codebase, there is nothing to compare and examine by a contributor, and hence nothing to comment or improve upon.

Hence, upgrades and contributions are usually done by highly skilled Java Developers adept at building games similar to Robocode.

If you are looking in any way to contribute or fix the Robocode game, either by installing features or via malware reports, the Developers Guide to building Robocode is a great resource for you.

Changes, however, are subjected to the terms and conditions already stated by OpenSource EPL

Robocode Modules

You can register yourself at the Robocode Developers Discussion Group to get help for Robocode internals and even kick off a new topic. One of the easiest ways of obtaining information and learning about the inner workings of Robocode is by striking a conversation on the Robocode Developers Discussion Group.

Contributions made to Robocode that are considered small often involve less than 10 files. The preferred way for that is the provision of said contribution as a patch file. The patch file can then be added or applied to the existing Robocode sources.

If the contribution is large, then a Subversion branch is made available for you to work with. Your additions and changes are then added to the Subversion, which will eventually be merged into the truck and examined by the Robocode administrators. The Robocode administrators might then make some adjustments to finalize the work.

CodeCombat

There are several ways to attract people, especially kids, to programming and nurture their skills as developers. One of the best ways to do that is to make the learning process fun and interesting for them. That will make them appreciate the process as well as engage them. Several coding games are designed to do just that. One of such games is CodeCombat.

More than kids, anyone interested in learning to code but is finding it difficult to master the basics, CodeCombat, with its full-on games and basic training, is the answer. The game enables beginners to master the various coding languages like JavaScript and Python with ease and in a fun and exciting manner.

The creation and introduction of CodeCombat has solved many of the learning problems that plague students by creating a way to pass information in an exciting and motivating manner.

CodeCombat was created in 2013 and it has, since then, been a great tool in expanding the knowledge of individuals interested in coding as it is making learning fun by letting them fight monsters, clear dungeons and complete quests.

What is CodeCombat?

A wise man once said "If you can't explain a concept simply enough for a child to understand, then you do not understand the concept". It was probably precisely this thought the creators of CodeCombat had in mind while developing the game.

CodeCombat is essentially the most modern and fun kid-oriented programming game ever created.

Set in the background of a traditional dungeon and adventure role-play, the game brilliantly employs the entertaining attractions of game playing to teach children the fundamentals of coding.

This is primarily done by ensuring that the characters in this game are specifically controlled by writing coding instructions in languages like Ruby, Python or JavaScript

Combing combat hack and slash role-playing with hard to crack logical quizzes and puzzles, the game is craftily designed to enhance children's interest and their programming knowledge with its dexterous mix of both fantasy and logic.

The movement of avatar characters in particular elicits kids' interest, as they can only move via code. When the proper coding instruction is written, the characters in the game correctly move, either by dodging or attacking. It need not be said that inputting the wrong code leads to unfortunate consequences for the characters

Like all games, CodeCombat is also stratified into game levels, with the complexity of coding becoming greater and greater with each stage. Eventually, kids who get to the advanced levels require a sound mastery of programming languages as it greatly determines then the outcome of the game.

Using CodeCombat in a Coding Curriculum

A truly amazing thing about CodeCombat is that unlike other regular programming games, it can be used solely and directly to teach kids how to code, right from the get-go!

The CodeCombat comprises 11 courses, all of which are thoroughly descriptive and contains numerous game levels for each course. To make things easier, the courses are divided and determined by the player's skill levels and age.

What the courses roughly covers are

- Computer Science

- Web Development

- Game Development

CodeCombat is teacher-friendly as well, in that it grants teachers the ability to pick out specific programs for their students from a general dashboard array of courses.

In addition, teachers are similarly granted access to personalize their lesson notes and adjust their course schedules, per their wards' progress, which is carefully monitored.

CodeCombat can also be used to master proficiency in a particular language, as the application offers programming translations, which come in handy when accessing the open-source community.

Why you should use CodeCombat to teach your kids coding, and why you should not.

Like a flipped coin, using games to teach coding can be viewed on two sides.

In some ways, using CodeCombat is advantageous, but it has its demerits also, the most obvious being that coding fundamentals are gamified and kids might not actually learn to apply these concepts in a more abstract sense. Another is the obvious drawback of it being suitable mostly for children, not adults. But anyway, enough of the cons. Here are some great advantages of coding with CodeCombat:

- **It's fun**

Right at the heart of it is the most obvious advantage of learning to code with CodeCombat - it's a game, not another boring lecture on abstractions.

Unlike other programming learning exercises, CodeCombat presents itself first and foremost as a game before anything else, which is tremendously attractive to kids. Rather than telling them straight on what is right or wrong, CodeCombat gamifies the whole experience and allows kids to remain entertained while studying programming.

Hence, children are not bogged down with undue panic and emphasis on what the right or wrong code is. Rather, they are more concerned about winning the game itself, which can only be done via inputting the right code. In a stroke, they both learn to code and have fun. Talk about a master coup

- **High Visual Gratification**

The traditional method of finding out there is a mistake in your code can be immensely frustrating at times.

Even in Java Note editors and games like Robocode, a poorly written code is rewarded, usually with the error message or an unresponsive screen. Which is cute at first, but gets frustrating after the first 150 times. Not so in CodeCombat.

Unlike other coding games, CodeCombat offers a highly visually explicit reason why your code is not working. You can see the source of the error, and why your command response is not being executed in real time.

This is immensely gratifying, and greatly encourages further development, especially for visual learners

- **Great Gameplay**

Of course, all the above advantages would be naught if the gameplay was crap. On that aspect, we can assure you of one thing - it isn't.

CodeCombat has an extremely attractive and skillfully built gameplay, replete with graphics and suave.

All the levels have been designed to be challenging enough for the players to keep them invested, but not too challenging that they give up at the impossibility of the task. There are also several hints available in scattered and varied locations designed to provide help to the players as they move along.

Like all traditional games as well, players have the freedom from scratch to pick whatever difficulty level they are most comfortable with and change it if they wish as the game progresses. On its own, the level of complexity in the game becomes higher and higher as well as the game progresses, making sure players aren't bored with it.

- **Simplified, Not Compromised**

Most coding games designed for children tend to have one nasty flaw. They always oversimplify concepts and make overgenerous exceptions, such as allowing even poorly written code to be executed. Not so in Code Combat.

CodeCombat is a simplified game that obeys the player's every instruction and can be easily understood by a novice who has no prior coding knowledge to get past every level. It ensures the players input the proper syntax commands and instructions, with the help of Brunner-friendly terms, and does not run coding command instructions unless their formatting, placement and basic structure is correct.

A good example is this:

The command, "hero.moveLeft()" instructs the character to move to the left but an instruction like "hero.moveLeft" or "heromove.left" veers the avatar straight right straight into the realm of spikes.

This might seem like meaningless pedantic corrections to you but every programmer knows the importance of correct syntax while writing code. A single improperly placed period, dash, parenthesis bracket can in reality be the difference between a proper coding instruction being run or an error message.

- **Great Community Support**

As we all know, one tree does not make a forest, and programmers do not grow in isolation. The great thing about the makers and fan community of CodeCombat is that they realize this too. There is a huge open source community for CodeCombatters on OpenSource, containing extremely helpful individuals always ready to lend a hand.

Accessing and Playing CodeCombat

As a "freemium" platform, CodeCombat encourages anyone to play for free without having to register or to create an account. With the 'Play Now' option available on their website, visitors on the CodeCombat site are immediately thrust into the combat zone. The character, armor and coding language can then be selected in the combat zone. The coding language options are JavaScript, Python or CoffeeScript.

CodeCombat was developed in Python, and hence is its home language. As python is generally regarded as one of the easiest and most effective programming languages to learn, the motto of the game which is 'Perfect for beginners. Simple but powerful' does seem to hold some water.

The other options of JavaScript and CoffeeScript, (which is basically regarded as JavaScript with finer syntax), are equally very important but easy to grasp languages as well.

With a rudimentary understanding of how those languages operate, children can commence playing immediately.

Opening an account on CodeCombat is 100% absolutely free, and an account, once opened, helps chart your learning progress.

For a schooling community, kids can be assigned Class Codes or can create an individualized account themselves.

CodeCombat Premium

As you know, almost everything in the tech World has an additional premium level. Hey, the developer's gotta eat.

However, unlike other platforms that start hassling you right from the get-go, CodeCombat is truly remarkable in that its first 11 levels are free of charge. That depth of playing is enough for you, or your kid to decide just how suitable CodeCombat is for your learning.

If you've decided CodeCombat is the one for you, or you still want to check it out more, you have to subscribe to play which costs 9.99 dollars (because 10 dollars is just too much!)

In addition to accessing higher levels, the subscription bonus comes with a host of other perks, such as 3,500 gems per month, useful for armor purchases in the game.

It can be canceled anytime as well.

The other perks that come with subscribing to CodeCombat include:

- A lot more missions.

- Additional lessons.

- Exclusive playable heroes.

- They will be allowed into the 'mage' class and the 'spellcasting' class, which provides more coding options.

Young parents and teachers with kids who love CodeCombat can greatly help their child's coding journey by investing in the game. Not only does subscription show you care about their developed, it also makes sure their already saved progress still remains, even after you cancel the subscription.

However, even without the 9.99 dollars, kids can still enjoy a lot on CodeCombat and the absence of a subscription is not some sort of disadvantage.

Gameplay

The gameplay is where CodeCombat truly shines.

Right from the get-go, fresh players are introduced to the fundamentals of coding languages and syntaxes, with a series of tutorials.

After that, each advancement comes with special levels singularly created for teaching users how to code by explaining how to move their characters via coding instructions.

Unlike the levels preceding them, these levels have no fighting missions or battling strategies, but instead contain simple, easy missions which allow players to focus on the coding instructions and understand how it works

To begin with, fresh new players only need to become familiar with these four commands:

- hero.moveRight()

- hero.moveLeft()

- hero.moveUp()

- hero.moveDown()

By using these commands to navigate selected levels, new players will begin to understand and become familiar with these four commands slowly. Next, new sets of instructions, all performable with tweaking already established commands are introduced into the game.

With steady gradual immersion, players who initially had no idea or skill in programming languages and how to use them start to attain steady proficiency at a carefully measured pace.

After clearing beginner levels, new players can then go on straight into the game and start exploring dungeons! Those already familiar with the language and the mechanics of CodeCombat usually skip the introduction levels.

CodeCombat is structured in a very vertical gameplay system. That is to say, it does not grant players the ability to explore dungeons and levels as they choose. Players can only move on to another dungeon after clearing all the levels in the order provided. For those who prefer exploring, or find the current level too hard, this might be a bit frustrating

Advanced Skills

As you progress through the game, the entire landscape changes. As the old saying goes, the higher you climb, the tougher it gets.

Each advancement leads to the introduction of more complex programming languages and higher stakes with a lot more specific instructions and orders, such as, "Clear a maze with only 7 lines of code, as opposed to the unlimited freedom you had as a beginner". Other concepts such as scripting and programming languages like HTML are introduced as well.

As you know, there are many levels of CodeCombat (over 400 in fact!), so clearing the game alone, a pretty immense task on its own, is bound to improve your game skills. It will also massively improve your coding knowledge, taking you from beginner to pro with a ton of fun along the way.

Verdict

CodeCombat is a programming game that everyone, especially kids, can benefit from.

It's relaxed and structured methods of teaching puzzling concepts in a frank, fun, and simple but not patronizing manner is one to be surely appreciated.

The game is simply amazing, especially in explaining complicated concepts such as variables and rational operators in an easy manner but without undermining what it is about.

CodeMonkey

CodeMonkey is another one of the coding games designed to capture the interest of children. Designed for kids who are 8 and above, CodeMonkey has struck the perfect balance between education and entertainment. While recommended for children 8 or older, those younger but no strangers to coding can also become patrons of CodeMonkey. Children who are also very quick on the uptake can also try their hands on CodeMonkey as there is adequate information available on the intricacies of the game.

While CodeMonkey is best used as a teaching device in the classroom, it can also be used by parents and guardians who wish to encourage their children's coding learning pursuits.

As CodeMonkey is better designed for the classroom module, it offers a teaching subscription complete with the necessary training and advised curriculum guide. This added addition is highly appreciated by teachers that lack the needed experience but desire to be involved in every step of their student's learning process. The curriculum and teaching guide ensures that the teacher is equipped with the materials and ready explanations for any confused student.

All teachers can monitor their students' progress individually via the provided dashboard and can inspect the code written by each of them. There is technical support available for teachers stuck at any point.

A unique feature that sets CodeMonkey apart is the language option available. Designed to be of help to more than just English speaking users. CodeMonkey is available in 18 different languages and is working on adding more languages. This will eliminate the language barrier and will make it even easier for non-English speaking coders to understand the concepts of coding easily.

Courses

With five different options to choose from, CodeMonkey has created a variety to match the child's preferences and keep said child engaged and willing to continue learning. The availability of options also ensures that the child does not get bored and can change courses as he or she desires.

Coding Adventure

Coding Adventure is CodeMonkey's main course. The course is filled with a variety of challenges, all of which are designed to entertain, engage and educate the children and beginners it is specifically designed for.

Coding Adventure makes use of a simple and easy to learn programming language called CoffeeScript. With CoffeeScript, the adventures are provided in a text-based format for players. This allows for the easy communication of the several core computer principles like loops.

Several adventures will capture the intrigue of teachers and students alike in various imaginary lands and exciting jungles. CodeMonkey has over 400 challenges, all of which are designed to cement the knowledge of the foundational coding concepts.

Game Builder

Another concept of CodeMonkey is Game Builder. Game Builder allows kids to test and explore their coding skills and better understand the topics of their computer science classes.

With Game Builder, students are able to:

- Build computer games of their own.

- Add their personal spin to the CodeMonkey games.

- Create interface games in swipe or touch that can work on mobile devices.

- Share their creations with all and sundry.

Game Builder's unique feature is that it is automatically assessed and self-paced. The availability of this feature makes it a wonderful addition in an educational setting.

Challenge Builder

For those who want a bit of a challenge or perhaps wish to let their creative side loose, there is the Challenge Builder which allows students to build their own challenges.

By building their own challenges, the students must have a sound understanding of the coding concepts as well as a good grasp of logical reasoning, creativity, algorithms and computer programming. The students need all of these in order to build challenges for themselves.

Challenge Builder allows its users to share their creative work with the rest of the world whenever they desire, just like with Game Builder.

Dodo Does Math

With Dodo Does Math, kids can learn to code and learn math at their grade level. This concept is directed at children who are still learning math at the 2nd to 4th-grade level.

By playing Dodo Does Math, the children make use of basic math concepts like addition, subtraction and distance measuring as well as the basic coding concepts to help get the eggs for dodo. Made up of 3 lesson plans and 20 challenges, this game allows real-time representation of their actions to allow the students to follow along quite easily.

Coding Chatbots

For the growing students, those who are or above the age of 13, CodeMonkey offers them Coding Chatbots. This game opens the door for the students into the world of coding.

By playing Chatbots, the students make use of the programming language, python, which they have learned with the game Snowman.

Chatbots have various advantages being beyond learning the coding concepts. It encourages the student's problem-solving skills and improves the critical thinking skills of said students. These skills are highly useful and will prove helpful to the student even beyond the realm of coding.

Computer Science Topics Covered

Just like all other educational websites, CodeMonkey has its own special focus and its specific approach.

Understanding the programming language used is the first step to learning with CodeMonkey. CodeMonkey makes use of CoffeeScript which is a great way of learning the more popular JavaScript.

Apart from the fact that learning with CoffeeScript makes it much easier to understand JavaScript, CoffeeScript also has its uses, mainly used for a web application. This makes a thorough understanding of CoffeeScript invaluable in virtually all industries. As CoffeeScript is similar to the way the English language is written, it is a lot easier and has a more friendly syntax than other languages, making it easily understandable for beginners and children alike.

CodeMonkey is designed to cover a wide range of computer science topics all through their various challenges. Among the topics covered are:

- Objects

- Function calls

- Loops

- Arrays

- Arguments

- Variables

- Keyboard and mouse events and so on.

Since the creators of CodeMonkey are constantly improving on the program, there are several new products introduced regularly. This is also something to look forward to.

Technical Requirements

Unlike some coding games, CodeMonkey is a web-based game that does not need software downloads. It can be played anywhere there is an available internet connection.

To play CodeMonkey on a laptop or desktop, the browser app used, like Firefox, Safari, Chrome or Internet Explorer must be up-to-date to ensure that the students enjoy their session on CodeMonkey. If the student is making use of a tablet instead, then said tablet must be relatively new. To ensure that the tablet meets the requirements, a rule of thumb states that the product must have been released in the past two years. However though, for tablets no matter how new, there are only about 165 challenges available. The skill mode challenges which are also available for tablet use also correspond with the challenges available.

Pricing

CodeMonkey has several payment plans available for the ease of your pocket and the plan that best suits the needs of the parents and teachers alike.

Homeschool

The homeschool payment option is created for private tutoring. It allows a ratio of 3 students to 1 teacher. Costing 109 dollars a year, this option offers 6 activities that have over 400 challenges. The activities make use of 3 math activities, one python course and 3 game builder courses. This payment method works best for a small gathering of children and ensures they have the teacher's undivided attention.

Super Teacher

Less expensive than the homeschool package, the super teacher package works best for a large gathering of people or a classroom. For 49 dollars a year, this package works for an unlimited number of students and allows 3 co-teachers. However, unlike the homeschool package which offers 6 activities, the super teacher package has only 1 activity which has only 30 challenges included. This works best for a large group of students as opposed to the homeschool package, which is only for a select few.

Custom School Plans

As the name suggests, custom school plans are created for schools that wish to include coding in their main curriculum. All CodeMonkey requires is a minimum of 20 students. It then offers a variety of packages which best suit the individual schools. Even as it offers the homeschooling package, custom school plans allow for multiple co-teachers. The cherry on top is the available personal contact to answer any questions or solve any problems that might be encountered as well as encourage the professional development of the instructors.

4 SQL Murder Mystery

The SQL Murder Mystery is a coding game with a more adult inclination to teach the intricacies of coding and its programming languages.

SQL Murder Mystery offers basic instructions at the beginning of the game. The instruction can be in this format:

"The detective requires your help to solve the crime that occurred. There is a vague recollection of a murder that took place on the 20th of January 2019 in the city of SQL. You begin your investigation by collecting all the reports pertaining to the crime from the database of the police department."

With that wonderfully mysterious opening, you're left alone to play Sherlock Holmes and find the culprit using nothing but your wits and your SQL query skills. Although experienced players night fine the game easier than complete beginners, it can still be pretty challenging at first. The whole process of identification and crime detection in itself is simply a brilliant way to teach you the basics of SQL while having some detective fun along the way.

SQL Murder Mystery is an immensely helpful game if you're looking to master the language quickly. With the aid of the game alone, you're going to be exposed to and have a better understanding of database concepts like Aggregate Functions and Table Joins, as well as understanding the distinction between concepts like Primary and Foreign keys.

The best part of SQL Murder Mystery is that it does not charge its users and it can be played anywhere and at any time in your browser.

Elevator Saga

Despite the saga tag, the actual gameplay in this game is a very simple and philosophically interesting one as well.

It starts off as a simple question - how many people can fit into an elevator if they optimized the space between them and continuously build from there.

The game is clear, simple, minimalistic, and very easy to grasp.

Filled with 19 challenges, Elevator Saga will teach you to adapt your algorithms to reduce the amount of time it will take passengers to move from floor to floor.

Untrusted

The game, which uses JavaScript as the main gameplay input, is browser-based and does not require software download. Untrusted makes use of a minimalist ASCII interface. The game requires constant edit of the JavaScript which runs the game to save a certain Dr. Eval from a confusing and dark reality.

Flexbox Defense

Ninth on the list is another game that employs strategy gameplay to teach you the essence of programming. But instead of robots and ships attacking this time, the game is more defensively oriented in that it's all about defending your tower from aggressors, hence the name Flexbox Defense.

Flexbox Defense is primarily a CSS focused game. It makes use of Flexbox commands, essentially a gameplay loop to defend your towers constantly against barbarian minions invading. The defense is primarily done by shooting attackers and employing other fiendishly violent options before they overwhelm the wall.

Ironically, for a game named defense, Flexbox Defense is surprisingly aggressive about teaching you the fundamentals of CSS and other general programming concepts. The game is the brainchild of Channing Allen, a master programmer seeking to make coding fun.

CodinGame

More of a collection of mini coding games than a single game, CodinGame is one of the best games to learn to code out there. Unlike many other games that can only be played in one specific language, CodinGame allows its players to code in whatever programming language they desire. The game editor has compiled and stored several programming languages on its server for your perusal.

More than its language options, CodinGame is also dedicated to keeping its players engaged with its built-in leaderboards as well as other additional features.

This program has been available since 2012 and not only is it still relevant to this day, no other coding game has come quite close. This game is available for free on any of your updated browser apps.

Chapter 4

Programming Languages

In previous chapters, we have discussed what programming languages are and how they actually operate as a bridge between human speak and machine language. We have also briefly mentioned the coding games that will help solidify your understanding of these languages and turn your learning journey into an extremely smooth, gamified experience. But what is the rationale behind these games and what concepts do they help you train, really?

Before the question is answered, first we must look at these programming languages themselves and briefly outline how they work. Only then can we understand the key concepts these programs rest on and how these games aid your programming journey.

In this chapter, we will introduce some basic programming languages and basically everything about them.

HTML

When talking about programming languages, it is only so proper to start from its forebearers, i.e., the very first of such language to be developed. And the very first language to be written for machines by humans for general purpose use is none other than the big one itself, the Hypertext Markup Language, otherwise known as HTML.

Sounds good, right? Except for one slight problem. Html is not regarded in some sectors as a true coding language. Why? This has to do with some factors described later in the five concepts of programming language (factors such as the lack of active functionality and dynamic variability).

In fact, HTML is regarded as more similar in organization and formatting to Microsoft Word than machine language per se, but so what of it?

It is still one of the oldest and one of the most popular languages used exclusively for web design and management. You can't ignore or escape using HTML. No matter how fast, how smart or how cool you are, if you really want to be serious with your programming language, HTML, like Thanos, is inevitable.

What is HTML and What Does it Do?
HTML, as I said above, it is an acronym for the term Hypertext Markup Language.

It is a programming language that gives users, i.e., programmers, the access to build and modify structured sections, titles and headings, embed web links and images, create quotes as well as paragraphs for websites, as well as internet applications. Basically every content you see on the web has, at its core, an HTML framework.

The language was originally created at the CERN research institute, you know, the one in Switzerland, by Tim Berners-Lee, whom you might also remember as the father of the internet.

His concept for HTML at the time was to facilitate the interconnectivity of the internet using a hypertext system.

And What is Hypertext?
Hypertext simply means embedded text, i.e., a text containing a link to another text, and can be viewed instantly by users, texts upon texts.

It's the very basis the internet is founded on.

Think about it.

When you open a Google search on your phone, it immediately shows you search results for your inquiry — a webpage. You then click your desired website, which then links you to the content of another website which you view instantly — yet another webpage. And on and on and on it goes.

The great true interconnected beauty of the web-based internet was only made possible through HTML.

And it's versatility has only gotten even more nuanced over time. With each new addition, the amount of features HTML supports has only grown more and more over time. It is not an exaggeration to say HTML is the most versatile web-based language right now.

How Old is HTML?
Like I said earlier above there, HTML is the first programming language.

The very first edition of the language was published in 1991, and it originally had just 18 HTML tags.

Ever since the 90s however, newer and more improved additions to the HTML language have cropped up and some old redundant features have practically become obsolete (i.e., no current browser supports these features). These new attributes are generally called tag modifiers, and they have greatly enriched the markup language.

In 2014, a new version of HTML was officially released by the World Wide Web Consortium (W3C) called HTML5. HTML5 contains close to a hundred tags and is currently the most recent edition of HTML there is.

How Does the HTML Language Work?
Files made with HTML language are called HTML documents. They are always suffixed with a .html extension. Html, like I've said above, is the language of the web, literally. Hence, they are accessed using web browsers (Edge, Chrome, Firefox, Opera, UC, you name it). All web browsers support HTML, and translates the content of your file into a viewable file for internet users.

On average, even the most basic website will contain many HTML file pages for different sections of the website, i.e., the "Welcome", "About us" and just the "FAQ" pages of a website will all be different HTML documents, without yet scratching the content body of said pages.

All HTML pages essentially consist of, or are built by using elements called tags. They are the most foundational hierarchy of the webpage. Tags create a structured system that organizes the contents and elements of a web page into order. Features such as paragraphs, quotes, images and links are all orderly organized using tags, usually inside another tag, and on and on and on, like a Russian doll set.

The orderly arrangements of tags inside one another are called nesting, and is a fundamental feature of almost all programming languages

HTML elements use the symbol <> and </> for opening and closing and closing tag attributes. It's a style of writing unique and peculiar to HTML alone.

A certain style, or distinguishable feature a programming language uses to express commands is called syntax. And the syntax for HTML is

Here is a list of all HTML tags. All of it is open-source and can be found on the world wide web Consortium.

Tag	Description
<!DOCTYPE>	This tag describes the type of document.
<html>	This tag defines the document as an HTML document.
<head>	This tag describes all information or metadata pertaining to the document.

\<title\> This tag is used to express what the document title or heading is.

\<body\> This tag is used to express or define how the body of the document should look like.

\<h1\> to \<h6\> These tags are used to define HTML headings for each particular operation. There are different types of headings appropriate for different situations.

\<p\> This tag is used to define a paragraph in an HTML document.

\<br\> This tag is used to define or insert a single line break in the content body of an HTML document.

\<hr\> This tag is used to express a new theme or a change of themes in the content body of an HTML document.

\<!--...--\> This tag is used to insert or express a comment.

\<acronym\> This HTML tag was used to express an acronym. It is now considered an obsolete tag as it is no longer supported on HTML5, the latest version of HTML.

\<abbr\> This HTML tag is used to insert an abbreviation or express an acronym in the new HTML5.

<address> This HTML tag is used to outline the personal contact information and details of the author of the article encased in the body content of the HTML document.

<b> Just like Microsoft world, this HTML tag is used to bold a text.

<bdi> This HTML tag is used for the isolation of a particular segment of the text for special formatting unlike the text around it, e.g., an intense quote.

<bdo> This HTML tag is used to override and change the direction of the current text in the HTML document.

<big> This HTML tag was used to make a text bigger. It is now considered an obsolete tag as HTML5 no longer supports it.

<blockquote> This HTML tag was used to highlight a segment in the content body borrowed or quoted from another work.

<center> This HTML tag is used to move a text to the center of the document. It is now considered an obsolete tag, as it is no longer supported in HTML5.

<cite> Like the header, this HTML tag is used to define and express the working title of a document.

<code> This HTML tag is used to outline a segment of computer code, ostensibly different from HTML.

<del> This HTML tag is used to highlight a text section that has been deleted from a document.

<dfn> This HTML tag is used to specifically highlight a term that will be defined in the content of the document.

<em> This HTML tag is used to highlight an especially emphasized text segment in an HTML document.

<font> This HTML tag was used to select the font, color and the size for the text appearance in an HTML document. It is no longer supported in HTML5.

<i> This HTML tag highlights a segment of the text in a different voice or mood.

<ins> This HTML tag highlighta a text that has been inserted into the body document.

<kbd> This HTML tag is used to define the input of the keyboard.

<mark> This certain tag is used to outline certain highlighted or marked text.

<meter> This HTML tag is slightly different from others. It is used in a more mathematical sense, i.e., it is used to measure a scalar quantity in the boundaries of an already give range or gauge.

<pre> This HTML tag is used to outline texts before formatting, i.e., pre-formatted text.

\<progress\>   This HTML tag is used to signify the progress of a task.

\<q\>   This HTML tag is used to describe a short quotation.

\<rp\>   This HTML tag is more backend programming inclined. It is used by web designers who code in Ruby as an alternate fail-safe in case a browser doesn't support the language. This HTML tag prompts what to show in cases of these browsers that fail to support ruby annotations.

\<rt\>   This HTML tag is used more visually, for the definition or description of characters in the East Asian typography.

\<ruby\>Like the tag above, this HTML tag is also for the East Asian Typography. It is used to define a ruby annotation.

\<s\>   This HTML tag is used to describe a text that was correct once before but no longer is.

\<small\>   The inverse of the \<big\> tag, this HTML tag is used to make a text in the body document smaller.

\<strike\>   This HTML tag was used to describe a strikethrough text. It is now an obsolete tag as it is no longer supported on HTML5.

\<strong\>   Just like Microsoft word, This HTML tag is used to define an important text and make it obvious

\<sub\> This HTML tag is used to turn text into subscripts.

<sup> This HTML tag turns text into superscripts.

<template> This HTML tag is used to specify or determine a placeholder or container where a content should be "hidden" after the page loads.

<time> This HTML tag is used to describe a specific timeline or date.

<tt> This HTML tag is used to determine the type of teletype text. It is now an obsolete tag as it is no longer supported in HTML5.

<u> This HTML tag is used to describe certain segments of text that are unarticulated and differently styled from normal text.

<var> This HTML tag is used to define a particular variable.

<wbr> This HTML tag is used to define a word or line break in the HTML body document.

Forms and Input

Tag	Description
<form>	This tag is used to input an HTML form for user action.
<input>	This tag is used to define input control.
<textarea>	This html Tag is used to create a text box or text area for multiple input control.

<button>   This HTML tag is used to create a clickable button in your HTML document.

<select>   This HTML tag is used to create a drop-down list of options in your document.

<optgroup>   An upgrade to the tag mentioned above, this HTML tag is used to create a group of related options in a drop-down list.

<option>   This tag is used to create an option in a drop-down list.

<label>   This tag is used to define a particular label for an <input> tag

<fieldset>   This HTML tag is used to classify group related elements inside a form.

<legend>   This HTML tag is used to create a particular caption for the <fieldset> elements

<datalist>   This HTML tag is used to specify a list of pre-defined options for input controls.

<output>   This HTML tag is used mathematically to express the result of a calculation.

<frame>   This tag was used to create a window in a frameset. It is now considered obsolete as it is not supported in HTML5.

<frameset>   This tag was originally used to create a set of frames in an HTML document. It is an obsolete tag as it is no longer supported by HTML5.

<noframes>   This tag was used as a failsafe to create alternate content for users whose browsers did not support frames. It is now considered an obsolete tag, as it is not supported in HTML5.

<iframe>   This HTML tag is used to describe an inline frame.

<img>   This HTML tag is used to insert an image.

<map>   This tag is used to insert a user access image map.

<area>   This HTML tag is used to describe an area inside the image map.

<canvas>   This HTML tag is employed in the drawing of graphics and other visual elements in the document. It is usually done with the aid of Javascript.

<figcaption>   This HTML tag is used to describe a caption for a <figure> element.

<figure>   This HTML tag is used to specify a self-contained content in figures.

<picture>   This HTML tag is used to define a placeholder container for multiple image resources.

\<svg\> This HTML tag is used to create a container for graphics with SVG functions.

\<audio\>   This tag is used to insert sound and audio content.

\<source\>   This tag is used to create different media resources for different media elements such as sounds, videos and pictures.

\<track\>   This tag is used to create readable text tracks for media sources such as video and sound.

\<video\>   This HTML tag is used to insert a video or movie into an HTML document.

\<a\>   This HTML tag is used to insert a hyperlink into an HTML document.

\<link\> This tag defines the relationship between the contents of an HTML document and similar contents that can be found in an external resource, such as a spreadsheet.

\<nav\>   This HTML tag is used to create navigation links.

\<ul\>   This HTML tag is used to create an unordered or random list.

\<ol\>   This HTML tag is used to create an ordered list.

\<li\>   This HTML tag is used to create a listed item.

<dir>   This HTML tag was used to create a directory list. It is now considered an obsolete tag as it is no longer supported by HTML5.

<dl>   This HTML tag is used to create a descriptive list.

<dt>   This HTML tag is used to insert a particular term/name in a list of descriptions.

<dd>   An alternate form of the above tag, this HTML tag is also used to insert a particular term/name in a description list.

<table>   This tag is used to insert a table in an HTML document.

<caption>   This HTML tag is used to insert the caption of a table.

<th>   This HTML tag is used to create a header cell in a table.

<tr>   This HTML tag is used to create and specify the number of rows in a table.

<td>   This HTML tag is used to create and specify the number of cells in a table.

<thead>   This HTML tag is used to specify and group the header content in a table.

<tbody>   This HTML tag is used to define the content in the body of a table.

\<tfoot\>   This HTML tag is used to define the content groups in the foot of a table.

\<col\> This HTML tag is used to group and specify the properties of a column for each column within a \<colgroup\> element.

\<colgroup\>   This HTML tag is used to specify a group of one or more columns in a table for formatting.

\<style\>   This HTML tag is used to describe the type of style information pertaining to a HTML document.

\<div\> This HTML tag is used to describe a section in the content body of a HTML document.

\<span\>This HTML tag is also used to describe a section in the content body of a HTML document.

\<header\>   This HTML tag is used to insert a header in the content body of a HTML document.

\<footer\>   This HTML tag is used to insert a footer in the content body of a HTML document.

\<main\>   This HTML tag is used to highlight the actual main content of a HTML document.

\<section\>   This HTML tag is used to insert a particular segment in the content body of a HTML document.

<aside>   This HTML tag is used to insert additional content apart from the main one found in the page.

<details>   This HTML tag is used to insert or subtract additional details that can be viewed or hidden from the user.

<dialog>   This HTML tag is used to create a dialog box or window.

<summary>   This HTML tag is used to create a visible heading for hidden content defined by the <details> tag.

<data> This HTML tag is used to add a lower level machine language readable translation of a given content.

<head>   The function of this HTML tag is to provide important details about the HTML document.

<meta>   This HTML tag is used to highlight the metadata information about an HTML document.

<base> This HTML tag is used to specify the URL location or base URL target of an HTML document.

<basefont>   This HTML tag is used to select the default size, color and font for the text in the document.

Programming

Tag	Description

<script>   This HTML tag is used to create a user access script.

<noscript>   This HTML tag's function is to show different contents for web viewers whose browser does not support web scripts shown in the content body of the HTML document.

<applet>   This HTML tag was used to insert an embedded applet. It is now an obsolete tag, as it is no longer supported in HTML5.

<embed>   This HTML tag is used to create a container for a foreign, i.e., (non-HTML) application or language in the content body.

<object>   This HTML tag is used to insert an embedded object into the HTML document.

<param>   This HTML tag is used to define the parameter specifications for an object.

JAVA

The next language we're going to examine is the most popular and widely used coding language in the coding world, Java.

What is JAVA?

What is Java? It is a name thrown often and a word repeatedly said in the coding world with the expectation that its meaning is quite clear. Well, Java is a computer programming language that serves a general purpose just like other programming languages like Python and JavaScript. Java can also be compared to C++ and C# because it is an object-oriented programming language. When Java was created, so was Java Virtual Machine which effectively turned Java into a platform. In JVM's early days, the only program that ran on it was Java making them quite interchangeable. The times passed and new programming languages were created. Some of these new languages like Scala, Groovy, jRuby, an implementation of Ruby, and Jython, an implementation of Python, can now run on the Java platform.

What Are the Origins of JAVA?

Java was created and released in 1995 by a team of visionaries at Sun Microsystems. It was subsequently sold to Oracle. The visionaries were inspired by the available computer programming languages such as C++ and C. This is the reason why there are a couple of correlations between those languages and Java. As the team picked out the features they liked from the available languages, they were also sure to discard some characteristics that have proven troublesome and difficult for the users of those languages.

The team believed their new programming language would be able to run on all consumer appliances. As forward thinkers, the team envisioned a world where a single chunk of written code would be able to run any and all household appliances such as the microwave or the refrigerator or what is now known as the internet of things. With the recent invention of those appliances that can run on code, it is easy to appreciate just how much foresight the Java creators had by building such a code in the 1990s. Java was designed such that users will be able to write a chunk of code that will be able to operate any electronic device anywhere and at any time.

Not everyone has the foresight that the creators had, and Java did not become widely accepted. Its creators then decided to take another approach. As the worldwide web was released at about the same time and has received a warm welcome, Java's creators decided to latch onto that. The creators had inputted a feature that allows for something called applets. Applets are small programs that could run in a web browser. Even though it was not the creator's plan, they decided to play smart and ride on the applet and world wide web wave into stardom and popularity. This is the reason why the majority of the web applications available today are written in Java.

Statistically-Typed vs Dynamically-Typed Languages
The typed languages are divided into two main types; the statically typed language, and the dynamically typed language. These two languages are quite different and have their individual advantages. Ruby, Python and JavaScript are examples of dynamically typed languages while Java is an example of statically typed language.

Most programmers have their preferred typed language, and they all have various reasons for sticking to their choices. Several programmers have insisted that it is better to have learned how to write code with a statically typed language before learning dynamically typed languages. They believe that the extra layer of code needed for statically typed languages allows the budding programmer to think carefully and also makes the variables a lot more explicit. It is also believed that learners who start their journey with statically typed languages find it a lot easier to learn a dynamically typed language than the other way around.

Dynamically Typed: For programming languages like Ruby and JavaScript that are a dynamically typed language, there is no need to specify what type of data you wish to input in a particular variable. Such variables are said to be dynamic as they can be anything from a number to a sentence.

Statically Typed: Unlike dynamically typed languages where anything can be set as a variable, statically typed languages like Java needs to know the exact contents of a variable. Statically typed languages set content specific variables such as variable A holding only numbers while variable B is for just letters. This then creates a structure that catches any programmer mistake even before the program is run.

Which Languages Has JAVE Given Rise To?

When JVM was created, a couple of other languages such as Scala and Groovy were also created to run with the JVM platform. There have also been arguments that Java largely influenced the development of C#. This argument seems valid because C# was developed after Java and has a great deal of similarity with Java. That being said, C# has also had a positive impact on Java and the two languages are constantly building the other up.

How is JAVA different from JAVASCRIPT?

Netscape created JavaScript in the mid-1990s and dubbed it LiveScript. Unfortunately, it was not very catchy and didn't capture the public's interest and the developers would like. They then decided to change its name to something similar to the latest coding language that was getting all the buzz then and dubbed their language JavaScript. Their plan worked and their language became quite well known. However, this does not mean that Java and JavaScript are the same. Really, the only thing that binds Java and JavaScript together is the fact they both get their syntax from the original C programming language. Other than that, there is nothing similar between Java and JavaScript. You will, however, find it easy to master JavaScript if you have a solid understanding of Java and vice versa due to their similar syntax base.

Which FRAMEWORKS Should I use with JAVA?

As Java was created to be a general-purpose language, it is easily adaptable to any environment. It can run on just about any machine like the Linux machine, Unix box, Mac, Windows or even smartphones.

Is JAVA a Good Coding Language for Beginners?

Java is a smart choice for the first language for budding coders. There are several reasons which support this claim and those reasons include:

1. As Java is not a relatively new language, having been around since the middle of the 1990s, there are several resource materials about the language and several books available to guide beginners through the intricacies of coding with Java.

2. Because Java is so old, it has a lot more users than any other programming language in the world. Just like the numerous available resource materials, there are several available Java programmers to guide beginners in a step-by-step journey towards understanding and mastering Java.

3. Java, just like many other programming languages available, picked their syntax from the C language. This makes it so much easier to master other languages once the beginner fully learns Java.

4. As an object-oriented language, the lessons which the beginners learn with Java can be easily transferred towards the mastery of the other programming language.

PYTHON

Remember how we mentioned above when talking about Java that there were programming languages with "looser" variable definitions, also classified as "weakly typed languages"? Well, finally you get to meet one. Its name, Python

What is Python?

Python, as officially described, is a simple, clear backend programming language with a very dilute learning curve i.e., it is very easy to grasp and learn, making it perfect for beginners and neophytes in the programming world. Like the languages mentioned above, it is a high-level script, meaning it has to be translated to machine code (bytecode) before executing a program. A compiler does the Python translation.

As stated earlier, python is a back-end programming language, meaning it is not useful for front-end developers like UI/UX designers. Python is however important for other projects. There are many useful functions of Python. Listed below are just two of them:

1. Creation of libraries and data sets: Python is very useful in easily accreting and transcribing a large amount of scientific information to electronic form. This function has made it immensely popular and well used amongst academia and science-based communities for scientific computing amongst others. Knowledge transfer is routinely done via Python Libraries, as the program makes it so easy to do so.

2. Although not a front-end language, Python is still very useful for website coding and programming. It is very commonly used to create databases and web requests for offline servers of website platforms.

Python is one of the most used programming languages in the coding world today. Proficient knowledge in Python is even unofficially regarded as one of the informal "requirements" back end developers must have in their CV, especially for start-up companies focusing on Machine Learning. And its growth is not stagnant. Programmer adoption of Python is expected to go even higher in the coming years. This is because companies such as Google, Facebook Yelp and even Twitter all use Python, to some degree in their web design.

The next question of course is why is Python so liked? To answer that we must take a brief look at the history of the language itself.

The Origin of Python

1989 was, in many ways, quite a momentous year. For those in Eastern Europe, it was the era of revolutions and uprisings against the Soviet Union. For those in Panama, it was the year Uncle Sam finally invaded. And for those in countries like Australia and Japan, it was the year the drafted proposals for the World Wide Web, the now eponymous www. first surfaced. All in all, it was a year when revolutions with far-reaching consequences that would echo in today's world were taking place.

One such revolution, albeit much more silent, took place in the computer space. It was initiated by Guido van Rossum, a Dutch computer programmer with a master's degree in Computer science and mathematics from the University of Amsterdam, Netherlands. At the time, van Rossum was working on developing a new altogether different programming language at the behest of the National

Research Institute (CWI) for new coders. That language was called ABC and, at the same time, he started designing a small side hobby project to keep him busy and occupied during Christmas when offices were closed due to the holiday season (some people just don't know how to leave work at work premises). His major aim then was to write a programming language everyone, even non-programmers could use with ease. As he was fooling around, he decided on a whim to name this hobby programming language of the name of a popular TV show at the time. The name of the TV show was Monty Python, shortened to Python. Yes, this same Python.

What Makes Python Special?

Now you must be wondering, what is it about Python that made it so unique it changed from being a side hobby to being one of the most widely used programming languages in the world?

Well, the answer to that lies in three main reasons, although there are surely others:

1. It allows loose typing

Unlike other strongly typed languages that demand the specification of the data type before you input your variable function, python doesn't care about that at all. It is much more flexible about the variable specification, hence the term "loosely typed". This feature grants Python much more flexible and thus much more widespread use amongst developers.

2. It has meaningful Indentation

One of the unique features about Python that makes it so appreciated is the fact that it made indentation, i.e., spacing a necessary feature of the language. Unlike other programming languages that didn't specify or care about the spatial arrangement of their code, a necessary feature of Python code is that it must be well indented. This ensures that coding symbols are written well-spaced from each other, greatly increasing its readable nature, unlike other languages where hundreds of lines of code can be crammed into one single page. Ironically, this idea of making indents necessary wasn't well received at first by programmers who thought it would make the language more difficult to use. Given over 8.2 million active developers use the language and organizations like NASA have praised Python for its meaningful simplicity, it's safe to say said Critics deserve a bucket load of loser pie. Or looser pie?

3. It encourages responsible programming

Finally, a key factor behind the popularity of the language is that it stimulates and challenges developers to be better versions of themselves.

Except for its compulsory indentation, Python is pretty laissez-faire about the rest of programming. What this means in essence is that the developer is in full control of whatever code he writes, either good or bad, and is solely responsible for ensuring his code is logically sound.

This freedom is pretty much a double-edged sword. While Python does offer full flexibility which makes its language syntax easier and its rules easier to adhere to, the lack of guidelines in itself means programmers will get no warning or error message from the program if they make mistakes.

The only warning they'll get is after the program is compiled at the end, only for an error message to pop up during execution.

This approach is a mixed blessing. While it is no doubt extremely frustrating to have to debug your code a million times, the understanding each debugging lesson offers is priceless. Only with Python can programmers truly know how good they are without relying on external help, and how much they rely on guidelines and error messages in strongly typed variants to code properly.

In the end, Python gives you the freedom not only to grow, but make mistakes and actually learn from them. These are but a few of the reasons why Python is so immensely popular in the programming world today.

There are many other programming languages available out there, so many in fact that we could write a whole book on them. However, all such languages are essentially variants of these mentioned languages. This is not to say learning those languages is not important, in fact some are even more important in some cases than the languages mentioned. Rather, this short expose on programming languages was simply meant to highlight which types there are and some of their other less known quirkiness.

No matter the language you choose, two things are sure - you will face some difficulties mastering it at first. So much in fact that you might come to hate it.

And two, after attaining sufficient mastery in it, you will come to look the language, or at the very least, *not hate it.* That in itself is a more significant victory, especially in the complex, sometimes confusing world of computer programming.

Conclusion

And so we come to the end of this book. It's been quite a journey, hasn't it? No doubt you must have learned a thing or two from this book. And if not, at the very least you had fun reading this. I hope.

At the end of it all, it is worth repeating that coding and computer programming can be very fun to learn once you understand the fundamental workings behind it. And the easiest and most fun way to understand this is by playing games designed to teach you those concepts

Whatever language you decide to focus on and whichever of the games you choose to master, always remember that programming, like any other skill, is one that takes time and dedicated attention to developing. No matter how many books you buy or how many games you play, you will not sufficiently master the principles behind these games if you don't take time to study them. It also bears repeating that while coding games are great, they are a supplement in themselves and not the main course. Generally, you need to learn to code properly, while using these games as fun but intellectually stimulating relief from the "horrors" of coding. It would not do only to play these games and declare yourself a coder. Not only is this dishonesty, but you also run the risk of being embarrassed by an actual programmer. The waters of learning how to code are open; drink deep or taste not the shallow spring.

Finally, I thank you once again for sticking to this book until the very end. Hopefully this book will make you a much better programmer, and the coding games will help you top the coding game. Till we next meet.

Sayonara!